The Map

The navigation and translation
to life & the human experience

by
David Dayan Fisher

ISBN: 979-8-3388-8089-0

Cover design by Patricia Krebbs
Book design by Wordzworth.com

Retep Nap Creations

The Map

The Author
David Dayan Fisher

David has experienced a roller-coaster wonder of his own journey through life. From his parent's hellish divorce, when he was three, hiding in dark places hoping the violence wouldn't find him, wishing he was dead, to all the twists and turns and ups and downs that got him to where he is now.

With much trauma, physical and emotional, he traveled the hide-and-seek of life to finally crumble and go within to find what he couldn't find outside.

Expelled from Hebrew classes, cub scouts, and high school, he then went on to drug taking and dealing in London's clubland. Hedonism was his religion. After suffering some serious side effects of taking so many drugs, he decided to heal himself with clean food, fitness, and walking away from the scene and people that fed his mayhem.

He cleaned up his life, and at the same time found his passion in the world of acting.

He trained at the Royal Central School of Speech and Drama, went to improv classes, and joined a theater company, all while working in event catering as well as auditioning and doing commercials, bit parts, and pop videos.

In 2001 he moved to Los Angeles and continued with his dream. After four years of more of the same as he did in the UK, he got his break in the hit movie *National Treasure*. He also achieved success and recognition in other worldwide movies and TV shows such as *NCIS*. Of course, he always played the villain, the bad guy, killing many, and dying many times. He then began his other dream to write books, movie screenplays, and paint.

As time moved along, now with his two new-found rescue dogs and the sudden death of his mother, his mild fame and fortune never seemed to be enough. He had started drinking again, and anger began to surface. This was the catalyst to dive inward. Continuing his acting, he started to read Eckhart

Tolle's books and then became greatly interested in the deeper mechanics of human behavior. Now with nearly two decades of studying motives and emotions in acting, he delved even further into the depths of the ego identity, the soul's perceptions, and all of the labels of consciousness and spirituality.

In 2017, he left the circus of Hollywood and moved to a small canyon town outside of Los Angeles to focus on his art and writing. He soon met a lady who was his muse and catalyst to enroll in a college to study spiritual psychology. There he studied, lived, and worked with his partner in doing as much inner work as he could, as best he could. All his childhood wounds and trauma began to surface. Unable, and not fully educated with the deeper understanding and tools needed, to see clearly and heal, his relationship fell apart.

It was then that he made the decision to dive even deeper, to become the best possible version of himself, dedicating his life to the study and healing of his now resurfacing darkness and pain.

He studied with numerous masters and teachers; took courses here, there, and everywhere; read non-stop; and cried, wailed, and died again and again.

Delving into the experience of his own hidden pain and moving into it, healing it, was now his passion and priority. But it also meant figuring out as much about why we as humans have come to this place and space in human consciousness.

This had now become his purpose in life. He has published and written numerous fiction books and kids' books and will publish a magical realism fiction book in 2025. An avid screenwriter, he has written eight movies so far.

This book, he says, is the book he wished he read two decades ago. He hopes to assist others as much as possible, to give them the tools and understanding to transform their own lives. Reading and studying are just intellectual knowledge, ten miles apart from the actualizing of ingesting, digesting, metabolizing, and embodying each moment of each moment in the experiment and experience of life.

David continues to assist his own journey, from moment to moment, evolving in his own inward and upward travels, as well as assist others in his personal one-on-one Evolutionist sessions.

With Gratitude

With this book I give thanks to all the great dead and living masters and teachers of history and of our present times, from the prophets of then, to the parents of when, as well as the assistants, authors, and all others who have brilliantly been part of the orchestration of this evolutionary leap in the elevation of human consciousness to deepen our greater understandings of life.

This book is simply a perception, an understanding of, a way of being and seeing.

Warning

These words can shift your consciousness and perceptions. If you are in a relationship, it would become a bonus to both of you to be on the same page and both read this book.

Disclaimer

The information presented is the author's opinion and does not constitute any health or medical advice. The content of this book is for informational purposes only and is not intended to diagnose, treat, cure, or prevent any condition or disease.

Please seek advice from your health-care provider for your personal health concerns prior to taking health-care advice from this book.

I will repeat certain aspects throughout this book as a constant reaffirmation of its purpose of providing a deeper ingestion of the understandings and perceptions.

Contents

Introduction
Life is a Mirror
Showing Us to Us!

I'm going to simplify thousands of years of wisdom, the systems in place, and the last century or so of psychology and science into a precise and easy-to-understand operating manual and map to life.

From the Indian Vedas, the biblical texts, and the understandings of the Kabbalah to the wisdom of the Buddha, the ways of Christ, and much else throughout history, we have been given wonderful insights and enlightening clues to how to operate the human experience.

The universe, our planet, and animals, plants, and humans are always evolving. The genius of our human achievements has proven us to be rather astounding creatures, even if we are brutally, ignorantly, destroying Mother Nature.

This book is about the inner evolution that is now required to bring us to the next level of understanding that will enlighten us and contribute to the healing of all our past blindness.

Know Thyself!

This is the most profound statement ever written. Many tried to give us the operating manual and map thousands of years ago, and their words were simply ways to navigate and translate the human experience. Unfortunately, these ways were twisted in translation, or even purposely hidden, and turned into something quite different to their truth.

We were given the map, and we have been getting lost ever since.

Once I was blind, now I can see. Once I was lost, now I'm found. I am not of religion. I am of its true essence and meaning; to rejoin to all that is. To come back to the actuality of truth, my essence, the unconditional lens of perception.

Only the Children Will Enter the Kingdom

The young child is liberated and free from the constructed ego identity and personality of the adult it grows into. Clearing the lenses of the perceptions that we have created from childhood is how we come to see and be who we truly are.

Who Am I?

I am a space, a vessel, a vehicle, as well as a construct, constructed onto and into that space. That which fills the space is my conscious or unconscious awareness of myself in each moment of every moment. I see life through the lens of how I see, feel, perceive, and believe myself to be.

To ingest and digest this information, metabolize it fully, and embody it and actualize it, will mean you literally have to dissolve and metaphorically and energetically die so that you are no longer who you think and believe yourself to be.

This confronts our very constructs of identity and how we have operated our whole life. This is simply an aware and evolved perception, compared to the collective, seemingly normal one.

It's a hell of a ride to get to our heaven.

CHAPTER 1

Before the Beginning

Before we begin, there is a before the beginning that affects us all.

From the biblical sentence "The Lord our God, the lord is One," from the Hebrew prayer, the Shemar, the ancient Indians, and the natives all over the world to the quantum aspects of the science of the unified field that says all is connected, all is one. There is no matter, just a mass of energy vibrating at different frequencies. Here we all are sitting and spinning on a seemingly round rock in time and space, in a vast universe thinking we are who we are, utterly separate and disconnected from everything. Being human is the greatest delusion and illusion we believe ourselves to be.

Whatever your beliefs, science is now bringing us closer to the truth of what actuality is. This is not the same as our own seeming, personal reality. When you truly investigate, there is far more than our human sensory equipment can sense. A dog lives in its own sensory world, a butterfly in theirs, and an ant, elephant, eagle, and whale in theirs. Yet we all live in our world totally experiencing our different experiences through our unique and individual sensory equipment and lenses. None is actually the whole truth, just our own subjective sensory version and perception in a world of billions of different potential versions and perceptions.

I am just a pinpoint perspective in a field of many other pinpoints, all somehow seemingly stitched and sewn together to operate accordingly. This is what we call nature, the universe. We are of nature and of the universe. We are not separate. This must be known of the self and fully ingested, digested, metabolized, and understood. What is separate is our constructed sensory self that believes itself to be itself.

Astrology, geometry, and quantum physics were not invented—they were discovered. They have existed since time began, and obviously before. The design of the universe, the unified field, is obvious and very apparent. We operate the human vehicle with sensory equipment only capable of computing a tiny fraction of light and sound. That in itself speaks volumes about what can't be seen or heard or experienced or known. Plants are now known to be sentient and sensory, able to communicate, have feelings, and assist each other. Their experience is just as real to them as we are to us. And in our blindness, we think they are just plants.

If I took all your senses away, you would still exist. You would simply be in the vast potential of conscious awareness. You would also simply have a load of software programs of your beliefs and thoughts of the past. They are not who you are, just memories and perceptions of your journey, of whom you became to be, thought you to be, and believed you to be.

So, all is connected, and all has its unique sensory experience, operating along its way in what we label a life. Quite the magic trick. They say we live in a simulation, a holographic experience, a computer game as such. Maybe we are not the player in our play, in our life, but the controller, the gamer of the player in the game, like a method actor acting out their role in a movie. But we don't know this of ourselves because we believe we are who we are, who we became. Know thyself.

Read the book *Metahuman* by Deepak Chopra for a mind-blowing scientific understanding of human mechanics and experience.

CHAPTER 2

A New Lens of Perception

L et's just say, what I'm about to write is just a theory. You don't have to become religious; you simply just accept it as a new potential idea of how to see life. Being able to do that, in itself, allows us to change our inner perceptions and have a broader, more expansive understanding. A perception is just that—a belief, a point of understanding, a way we see life. And if we look back at our life, we have constantly altered our perceptions from the time when we were a baby, a young child, a teen, and an adult. You have picked up this book for the very reason to broaden your potential perceptions.

You are a soul taking a ride in a virtual reality theme park, and you are using a human vehicle. You are the actor, the gamer, and you are the character you play. And you're doing this to partake in the experience we call life, to grow, to meet certain teachers and learn certain lessens to find your way back to the truth, to love, and to have a crazy human ride.

Life can actually be seen and lived as a school. And the soul's perception is labeled as the unconditional. It has no humanness to it, but that of the highest form of love. We have called this enlightenment "Christ consciousness" and given it many other human names and labels. It is a state of being and seeing, a higher perception, a greater understanding, that stands above all our normal, ordinary, programmed, and conditioned human interpretations and beliefs. Much of the world actually has these beliefs. But they think we are a human that has a soul, instead of being a soul who has a human.

We all have the potential to go from the ordinary to the extraordinary, from a basic unaware, blind, and unconscious mind to the insight of an enlightened, highly aware, and evolved conscious mind. We all have the potential to become alchemists, baby buddhas, or unconditional Christs in training. We are born into the brilliant sea of potential and possibilities, which many humans have repeatedly proved over time and history.

We use our human sensory vehicle and have a specific individual and unique journey and curriculum tailored to us, in the school of life, with lessons to learn, all set out for us, and we have all the tools within us to come to this higher seat of being, knowing and seeing. Yet, thousands of years of misinterpretations of the human operating system have blinded us to this way, to the use of the Map.

It's like we all need to have a serious software update to learn how to operate our experience with a clearer view, with fewer blind stumbles, tumbles, falls and sufferings.

"To be in this world but not of this world." A quote from Christ, a man of love.

"Nothing is real. And nothing to get hung about." A quote from the Beatles.

These two statements, two thousand years apart, describe the journey I am about to take you on. It means to be living in the world you have always lived in but being able to begin to see it in a very different way to how you normally have, and how most others still do. It will allow you to find peace where you once found yourself fighting with life.

CHAPTER 3

Life Is a School of Mirrors

All events, circumstances, situations, and people are there to reflect us back to us.

Let's just say, for the theory and practical practices of the Map, as tiny babies we are unconditional beings. We have no idea of our gender, our conceptual constructs of identity, our character, and our personality, and we have no beliefs of who we are, or perceptions or understandings as yet. We are a clean slate, so to speak. And yet, we are fully us, nothing more and nothing less. We are pure and authentic beings of joy, love, and giggles. We can't really get upset and disturbed and triggered like adults because there is no ammunition in there to get triggered from. Our basic machinery of our biology is survival and safety, with a built-in fight or flight stress response.

At this point, we then move into the school of life. We don't know our name but are still fully us. We don't know if we are a boy or a girl and don't know all the messiness that comes with that aspect of our future constructed idea of self, but we are still fully us. We don't attach ourselves, or identify with, or get stuck to labels of religion, nationality, politics, skin color, race, or anything else relating to human identity. And yet, we are still fully us, who we are. This is our essential, true, authentic self. This is who we all are under the conditioning, programming, thoughts, and beliefs of who we think and believe we are.

Let's say that our first reference point is love, or a clear and untainted loving awareness. OK, maybe add feelings of hunger and an odd feeling of needing to burp, fart, pee, and poop. For most of us, breastfed or not, we were held, comforted, loved, and secure, naked on our mother's flesh for much of our inception time while babies. What perfect bliss this must have been to feel so accepted, held, safe, warm, and fully, unconditionally, loved.

This was our immaculate inception imprint of the ultimate feeling: loved, safe, and secure.

Soon enough we become bereft from the breast, as I say, to then have to become who we became, to fit in, to be OK, to feel accepted, to survive, to feel safe. I will get to all this soon enough.

As we move into our childhood, we begin to build the human personality, our very own personal reality, our ego, our character, and identity from within, by our interpretations of our circumstances and the people around us and information that informs us.

It is we, from inside us, who build our beliefs and thoughts about us.

From these interpretations we inform our self-perceptions and ideas about ourselves. And these constructs are what we believe ourselves to be, the story of who we think we are, and we then live from this constructed, self-created character. This is the formation of our human ego identity. If I have an ego, have an identity, it's something I have constructed, not something I am. I was already me before I became that me. I am the essence, the foundation that my ego and its identity were built onto and into.

If we think about it, and we do quite a lot of thinking about a lot of things a lot of the time, can we actually hear our thoughts, the stories in our head, our fears, our inner critic, our inner judgments about ourselves? Yes! We are usually, mostly, unaware of being aware of them. This being said, who is it who is aware of us thinking when we do see the thoughts? Who is the awareness, and who is the thoughts and feelings I have and am aware of?

I am not who I think I am. I am the awareness of who I am. I am the actor who sees and knows the act, the gamer who knows and plays the character in the game. They are not one and the same.

Now I am already in a greater expansive space of myself just by knowing this of myself. This is called my conscious awareness. Most of us have spent our whole lives unconsciously unaware, thinking we are who we are, that we are our identity, our thoughts, feelings, and beliefs. Remember, our little baby was pure and innocent, simply a bundle of conscious, loving awareness, a space of potential and possibilities, a foundation of essence, love, and not much else. Then we stuffed that lovely space full of stuffing.

CHAPTER 4

The Patriachy

This labeled system of thousands of years of human conditioning, the patriarchy, has a cause and effect that lives in our underbelly. Most don't even think about it, because they simply live inside its constructs, not knowing any different.

All the men of humanity, the masculine, were once a small boy. And this small boy was natural, authentic, sensitive, and vulnerable in his essence, his truth. As he grew up, he had to alter his nature to become the human, patriarchal, conditioned idea of a man. He was told that men do this, men do that, men don't do that, be a man, man up, and all else that then cloaked, clothed, and covered his authentic child.

He had to become part of the system, and how others wanted him to be.

Mostly, his authenticity, sensitivity, and vulnerability were pushed aside to become tougher, stronger, more competitive, and more manly to fit the mold of a man. Being emotional was not acceptable.

A little boy trying to be a man, with a manly father, surrounded by people telling him to be a man, with manly heroes all over the media, now literally has to perform to be what he's not capable of being, because he's still just a little boy. And this creates a lot of deep inner shame, with deeply hidden feelings of not good enough ness. And that shame also has to be hidden by the little boy. That is all squashed down with all the rest of his natural feelings and emotions he's not supposed to show or feel.

To compensate, the sensitive and vulnerable little boy becomes like a cartoon character of his truth, trying to be what he's not, pretending to be what is demanded by the world and all those around him. And if not, if he can't be as the system demands, he becomes a lesser self, feels less of a man, inept, not good enough, living in his inability to match up to what society deems correct manliness. He now believes and owns his unworthiness, doubts himself, and lives in this deep feeling of lack and shame.

The other little boy, who does all he can to be a manly man, becomes the man boy he's been told and cartooned to become. He becomes competitive, gets defensive, and overcompensates by varying degrees, with passive-aggressive tendencies, striving to prove himself, gaining attention, approval, and external validation to feel like a man, in a world of men and other little boys also trying so very hard to be men.

Now he's always on guard, always trying to be something, someone, somehow more manly. He is a machine of pride that he claims and hides in. He's a bad actor in a world of cartoon actors we call men. And he operates under this constant pressure of fight or flight survival. The man is trapped in a trap they don't even know they are trapped in. There are now two types of patriarchal men. The one who is just not good enough or manly enough, and the one who constantly tries to be manly and good enough. Both come from the same place of a little boy who feels not good enough, and the huge amounts of hidden shame of feeling so. One wallows, and the other overcompensates. One lives in shame, the other hides it.

The little boy is also raised by a mother conditioned into the same system, who was raised by a mother and father of the same system. There is now a heritage of unknown patterns playing out for thousands of years. And most little girls are raised by these little boys who grow up to be their fathers. And these fathers, who are mostly void, to a degree, of their emotional intelligence, sensitivity, and vulnerability, are also mostly absent in time and space in the day, through no fault of their own, due to the effects of having to be a patriarchal man in a nuclear family. This has a huge cause and effect on the little girls.

The little girl naturally looks to her father to learn to feel safe, to feel fully met emotionally, to feel secure, and so fully loved. The little girl is also not allowed to show certain emotions, or share them with her father or patriarchal mother, because this is usually seen as being too much, too loud, too sensitive, too emotional, and they have no idea how to cope, how to meet her where she is, and be with her that way, because the parents have also been conditioned into their own effects of the patriarchy for eons. Children are hushed, quietened, told not to be loud, told this, told that, told and told, because we simply only know this is how it should be. This translates to all children to restrict their emotion, that it's not safe to do so, to be so, to be them.

So now we have a whole world of mostly repressed, confined, conditioned, suppressed, cartoon humans playing their programmed play. And when many of these little girls grow up to seek a partner, all that is out there is a patriarchal pool of men raised by the same system. She then tries to get the depth of love, the emotional vulnerability she never got from her father, from a bunch of men who can't give it to her.

The bridge between the masculine and feminine is basically blocked and broken by this false conditioning. We have been perfectly divided. Little girls and boys of the patriarchy are raised into a heritage of inauthentic, over-masculine cartoon men and defensive, unsafe, and overtly protective masculine women, all seeking security where it mostly can't be found. The little girl also grows up in her own soup of the last century of the effects of the patriarchal male-led machine of the media, with all its comparisons and mind manipulations. This has been created by stealth on many levels to breed a deep feeling of not good enough ness and insecurity.

We now live in an over-sexualized, overtly vanity-driven system built by stealth to create deep emotional insecurity, keeping women comparing, competing, and conditioned into their unsafe not good enough ness, with men striving to be more, show more, and think they are more, or wallowing and getting stuck in their own shame of not good enough ness.

This creates trillions of dollars from the skin-deep shallows of the design and its effects. The woman has been manipulated to use her face and body as a sexualized weapon.

Go to the natives and indigenous people of this world; they suffer none of the neurotic vanities of our society. The patriarchal media parades and objectifies the woman, has the men dribbling like fools, and blinds them both into their constant of a staged play of a disconnected and wounded hide, need, and seek. The distance between the two sexes has been created by stealth and should not be so far apart.

The Nuclear Family

For eons, near on millions of years, humans and our ancestors lived in communities, tribes, a village, full of support, safe and sound in this very natural design. In addition to a father and mother, there were always eight other aunts and uncles, a ton of grandparents, and an array of other children of all ages to be with, hang with, play with, and be in nature with. There was no single-parent pressure cooker with no support. There were no frustrated parents desperately trying to get by with only themselves to cope, with one of them going off to work all day. There was very little, if any, heritage of not good enough ness, wounding, or trauma, passed down in comparison to the nuclear family unit.

Tribal people of this world don't suffer the amount of neurosis and emotional baggage that we do. Their children grow up with the constant of mature adult energy and are not separated into ages, to then be with just their immature peers as examples and influences. That one aspect of the nuclear family society, on its own, creates a huge need of trying to feel accepted, approved, validated, and loved. Many studies have been done on tribes and communities around the world. They literally don't suffer the diseases we do, the addictions we do, the crime we have, and the depression and suicides we keep experiencing in ever increasing numbers.

We think it normal to shout at children, scold them, punish them, hit them, and generally put our tempers and frustrations onto them. We pressure our kids to perform for us, be how we want them to be, as an extension of our ego, for us to feel good, and from a hand-me-down, unknown conditioning our parents and society play out on us. I call it the ten thousand wounds of every child.

The always being told, always being made to be quiet, repressed, always being shown how others wanted us to be, all add up to a bundle of inner abandonment issues as well as a nervous system that is stuck in a constant state of fight or flight survival to just feel safe. Any words uttered out of the softness of love cause serious effects to the sensitive child's perceptions and psyche. Remember, the baby starts from love. From then on, all is interpreted as unsafe and not loved.

Then, soon enough, the child has to perform for cookies, to get gold stars and grades, sit in lines in classes, and then learn a load of stuff that is stuffed into them, without regard for their own individual unique needs and talents.

If you are not up to a set standard, you feel lesser than. If you can't perform well enough, you won't be loved or validated enough. This very pressure of the system of the patriarchy, nuclear family, schools, the media, peers, religion, and culture create and constantly perpetuates an underbelly of deep subconscious, unconscious, unknown programs and beliefs of lack, unworthiness, insecurity, un safeness, and a general unloved, disconnected, not good enough ness. We all have these, to varying degrees.

Dysfunction has now become totally normalized. Dysfunction is not a bad word. It's simply the opposite of functioning well. It's not wrong, it just is how it is, how it's become. Virtually every child has been affected by the patriarchy and single-parent nuclear family systems and all else that supports it, educates it, sets examples of it, and so perpetuates it. Our personalities, emotional intelligence, and ego identities, who we believe ourselves to be, are now all constructed from the ten thousand wounds of the dysfunction of the old operating system of life.

We, as children, interpreted, as best we could, from our inception imprint of love, our misinterpretations, which then constructed our very own misperceptions, which created all the barriers of limiting beliefs we set inside us, into our bag of feeling unloved and not good enough. We believe and think ourselves to be who we believe and think ourselves to be, by our very doing, from us.

We did it. We, by us, made up the beliefs about us. No one did that but us. This must be deeply understood.

Our parents played out their parenting, their unconscious, unaware conditionings and patterns, their labeled dysfunctions, their wounds and traumas, their childhood hurt and pain and had zero idea that's what was happening. They did not know this of themselves. They were operating blind and uneducated, as it were. The sentence "forgive them for they know not what they do" is all about this. And this has to be seen, understood, ingested, and digested to be able to find a deep compassion and a greater understanding of ourselves, especially for our parents and others. There are very bad behaviors being played out on innocent children. This is not being denied. And yet without seeing the blindness and pain of the parents that do this, we will then carry our own weight of the poison behind our own judgments and resentments through life.

We are all effects of our own causes that seemed to be from others. Others play out their unknown wounded hurt and pain in their behaviors, and we grow up interpreting them, from an origin point of love, to then create beliefs and perceptions of ourselves that we are not good enough, not loved, unsafe, or not worthy of love. We also play the victim that they did this to us, and they did that to us. And that's how we remain as we grow up, in this victim state, and remain wounded, not good enough, and abandoned inside. This is one of the toughest pills to swallow.

Our parents were two people who did their best, where they were, how they were. How we are, what we think about them, how we feel about them, and about ourselves, and the past, is our own self-created and interpretated baggage, our chains, our blindness and constraints we have dragged along with us through our lives. What happened has long gone. They were how they were and are how they are.

We can't take back time or change them. But the poison we keep feeding ourselves about them and about ourselves because of what happened, because they won't be how we want, is all our doing. This is what they call taking full and utter responsibility and accountability for our own operating systems, our own beliefs about ourselves, and not be a victim and blame others, or feel unloved, unworthy, and unsafe.

Our parents' hurt and pain from their past, their childhood, was being played out, what we call projected, onto us. They had no idea what lived inside them, how to control it, and they simply didn't know how to operate their way out of their own pain. Just as we are now stuck in our own pain, they are the same and were the same. This is what the wisdom of compassion is. You are reading this book to obviously find a way to operate yourself out of your deep hurt and pain. Our parents didn't have these options or understandings.

If we can come to a greater and deeper understanding, we find our liberation and the elevated emotional and mental gifts of compassion, forgiveness and a far greater peace and grace than if we did not see it this way. The deep work to heal these wounds and pain is not easy and means learning more about how and why.

Why carry anything but that of a more peaceful, evolved, and loving compassionate life?

Forgiving Them and Us

Do we agree that your parents had a tough childhood? Do we agree that they had no training, no understanding, no way of knowing about their hurt and pain from their own dysfunctional background? Do we agree that they also wanted to feel loved and not get the opposite? Do we agree they must be and must have been full of hurt and pain? Do we now see that they did their best with what they knew and also with not knowing what they didn't know? Forgiving them is the first half of the liberation to our next chapter in life.

Can we see that they are just adult wounded children, who were once not mum and dad, but were just like you, fumbling through life without a map or any understanding of any of it? Can we accept this of them, then and now? Because we can only be in the disease of resentment, anger, hate, and pain if we don't accept these facts. And the anger and resentments we feel are just the little child inside who wanted and still wants love.

Just Love Me!

I have forgiven some serious deeds and much more from my past. I understand there are very unsavory behaviors. But underneath all of it, believe me, even though you don't wish to believe it, there was love, they loved you. They just had a very fucked up way of showing it.

OK. Now to the understanding that they didn't make us feel anything, we felt it, interpreted it from the imprint of love, and so created beliefs that we were unloved, unworthy of love, unsafe, not good enough, and generally believing ourselves to be lesser and no good. We created the stories and feelings about them and held onto them. And we created beliefs and stories about us and held onto them. Now we hold beliefs, feel these beliefs, think these beliefs, and our whole body owns these stories and beliefs and clings to them and stores them in our constructed wounded ego identity and its secret subconscious.

Here we are now, stuffed with our own stuck stuff we built and constructed, through no fault of anyone but our innocent child.

OK. That's kind of setting the scene for the actor, the player of the game, in the school of life, with a shit ton load of added stuff of weight and darkness. This is now the journey to enlighten us about all of this.

CHAPTER 5

The Womb

In the womb we are mostly unaware of our body, have no formed mind, and yet are totally aware of our essence of consciousness. We don't feel ourselves because we are floating in the same temperature as ourselves. This is the basis of a float tank. We are mostly, simply, the brilliance of being in the being of our being. And yet, it has now been proven that how our mother was, mentally and emotionally, how her relationship was with our father, or just as she was while carrying us, caused a soup of chemicals she shared with us. Our chemical makeup and our nervous system were already being formed before we are born.

If parents were shouting, the baby would literally take the stress and anxiety on via an osmosis of the fluids being fed through the lifeline, its nervous system, and energetic resonance. These micro messages constantly flowed in, informing and embedding into the construct of the future of the child's unconscious operating systems. Other than this, we were mostly in a bliss of being, a full potential, a blank slate, a virtual unconditional being. We could go into past life karma, but that's also another idea you can choose to add to the constructs of the human experience. As I said at the beginning of the book, I'm making this as simple and easy to ingest and digest.

Months of weightlessness floating through consciousness was how we all spent the beginning of life.

Birth

Imagine floating in bliss, no mental construct, nothing to think of, and suddenly you are squeezed, you feel pressure for the first time, you become aware of yourself, and you are pushed from all sides in darkness, constricted, squashed, and then pushed out into the world. Bam! Sound, light, feelings, and sensory overload become you.

And ACTION!

The movie of you and your life begins. Trauma could very easily be a descriptive word for this initial entry into the world. But soon enough, hopefully, we are held by our mother. The heartbeat that was our drumbeat and mantra for nine months in the womb now finds us again, at the breast. The warm flesh of our mother on our naked fresh flesh holds us like a lover's hug, back to the near bliss of the womb, and we are again held, met, and comforted into the unconditional.

So here we are, born, an authentic, pure, mostly clean slate of potential, free of personality, character, and identity, free of perceptions, and imprinted with the initial inception experience of the unconditional breast, or flesh, with maybe varying degrees of deep, hidden, unknown nervous system programs and a soup of chemicals that have formed our mother's journey through her pregnancy.

In the Beginning

Now we are born, and our whole system kicks in. We are literally like a sponge soaking up everything around us. We are computing and filing away all we can to somehow come to some understanding of the outside world. When you gaze at a baby, they live in this wonder, this joy, this loving amazement at the brilliance of the experience they have entered into. Everything is new, exciting, untainted, an amazement of nonstop information. We literally inform ourselves, by ourselves, from our sensory equipment and input.

Tones of softness and gentleness should be the normal from our caregivers. And yet, each of us comes into a nuclear family home with varying degrees of very different experiences. Let's just say for the purpose of understanding the school of life, we all start from the unconditional imprint, the love we feel at the breast, the peace we mostly lived in inside the womb. We are simply a loving awareness. From this point on, as I phrase it, we will slowly but surely become bereft of the breast.

Many and most of us were then subjected to the tensions and frustrations from the pressure of the nuclear family and all else our parents had to contend with. A newborn always changes the homelife, even if other children are present. Divided attentions always cause their effect. A newborn baby will always take attention away from other siblings who could then interpret this as a form of abandonment of love. And it can also turn the other way, when the other children get attention, due to the nuclear family cause and effect, the lack of other support from the should be tribe, the baby gets neglected to a degree, from moments to minutes, or maybe more, and so they interpret it the best they can, and is usually a feeling of not safe, being unloved, and fear.

Just one experience of being left by a mother, screaming for a few minutes, can create fear and abandonment in a baby, which sets the nervous system into fight or flight. We have computed and interpreted every tone, facial expression, word, and especially the energetic output of our parents and home. The sleepless nights of the parents, trying to cope with all else, fray the normality of the ability to keep patient and not get frustrated. These energies are also read by the child as unsafe.

As language becomes part of life, these constants of how others are around us infect and affect us, as we do our very best to interpret their ways as best we can from our innocent understanding, from a reference point of the unconditional. We cry for feeding, cry to be changed, and cry to be held and loved, to feel safe.

The more we don't get met, the more we feel unsafe, the more our nervous system starts to build around this. In a tribe, a community, there is always someone at hand to assist and take over. There is hardly any pressure to be felt by the child. The child is mostly always attended to, always met, always seen and always heard.

Even when a TV is switched on, the child would be unknowingly neglected of the potential parent's attention, communication, and presence. TV is not human nature, not human contact, or natural for a child to be subjected to. The child would seemingly be occupied, and yet, would have a light box to replace human contact and human emotional interactions. The great electric nanny has been the parental replacement for all of us.

This stimulation then adds to our nervous system dysregulation and plays with our attention span.

Parents do the best they can knowing what they can, what they know, to cope in the nuclear unit, as best they can. No one is to blame. All the tensions between parents, and between parent and child, will also play out as an energy that the baby senses and then has to navigate.

An unstable environment, which is quite normal because it is a nuclear family in the patriarchy, will create imprints and issues in the child's nervous system. And as the language of verbal communication continues to be learned, tones and voices change from soft baby talk to a very different kind of information.

Frustrated, stern, angry, impatient, tones, and many other negative reinforcements of No! Don't do that! Stop that! and much else constantly ring in the child's ears and into its mental and emotional construct and software of its subconscious development. Again, by varying degrees, a child before seven years old is extremely sensitive to all around it that is not loving. Up until seven, they live in theta waves in their minds, a virtual hypnotic state.

From the womb and the breast, the unconditional, we are now having to deal with all kinds of aspects of survival in many degrees of circumstances. Any raised voices to the child, or from the parents to each other, are literally interpreted as an unsafe and unloving space and place. Any scorn, shout, and aggressive physical contact is translated as the same. And this now becomes a minefield of short fuses, frustrations, anxieties, and constantly being corrected and told from our dependents how we have to be for us to feel approved of, accepted by, validated, loved and so feel safe.

Without any understanding of the hardship of the nuclear family, the stress of it all, the innocent unconditional baby soon enough interprets and learns a whole bunch of beliefs and perceptions about itself and its caregivers.

We have to behave how someone else now wants. We have to do as someone else now wants. We can't be this, do this, or a be that. We are literally having to become someone else, just to feel safe.

We start to form our personality from how others want and wish. We start to literally forsake, negate, neglect, and abandon who we were to become who our parents want us to be for them. We unconsciously, unknowingly, play out a whole range of plays to fit in, to feel safe. We do our best to be what others want, and at the same time we still struggle to be who we are because we have now become lost and blind to who we actually were, our authentic unconditional self.

From the breast, being fully accepted, approved of, validated, loved, held, comforted and safe, we are now trying to navigate our childhood and language and other's temperaments and wishes for us, while we try to squeeze into their specific designer box. We enter into what is known as intermittent reinforcement. We get snippets and scraps of love and validation when we're good, do as we're told, and neatly fit into their box. Most else is the constant of the opposites, punishment, being told off, told no untold times, told to do better, be better, shouted at, judged, criticized, or even beaten, or worse.

Now, we are actually two children. We are the authentic, unconditional, fully loved baby, and the now conditioned small child who has created their own beliefs and perceptions of feeling unloved and unsafe and not good enough that sits on top of our unconditional.

And this divide of the self is now in a constant battle to feel safe, to try to become fully loved again. We are bereft of the breast, conditioned out of the unconditional, and interpret and then create a boatload of barriers of beliefs about ourselves due to others and their behaviors. And most of these beliefs are not the fullness of who we could be, but mostly a limited and unloving perception of how we feel about ourselves compared to our old brilliant and full whole truth.

We are now living with fear, unsafe and in fight or flight survival, trying to feel safe in between snippets of love.

We push aside our emotions, our feelings, and hide them so as not to be too much for our caregivers. When we do emote our feelings or our pain, we are hushed, quieted, told not to be so sensitive and not to be so emotional. We, from within us, literally interpret this as "it's not safe to be me, as I am," and so we cement and perpetuate a constant of our abandonment of our authentic emotional self.

It seems like we are loved for who we are, but we are only loved for how others want us to be, how we play it for them.

Our truth, our fullness, is too much for our parents or caregivers, and so interpreted by our small child as not good enough. And because of this, our actual self feels unworthy of love, unsafe in life, and constantly trying to feel loved and safe and worthy by being this other version.

This is our deep inner pain of our self-inflicted poverty, our abandoned self, the child begging for approval, acceptance, love and validation. This is the underlying pain of the unloved self.

To get a cookie, we have to be good and do well. To get praise, we have to fit in. To feel of value, we have to perform to be so. And all this keeps reaffirming our authentic true self that we, as we are, are not good enough, not worthy as we are, and not loved fully for who and how we are. We willingly, and unwillingly, accept conditional love out of the need for survival, to feel safe.

We all now have an unloved child inside us who just wants to be loved for who it is. And this is a deep hidden hole of pain we then carry within us and with us. These barriers of beliefs block our essence, our truth, and we are now programmed and conditioned to seek outside of us for love and value. And this imprisoned self then forms a constant ache and pain inside to feel fully loved and safe again.

Through no fault of theirs, most parents simply just tell children what they tell them. They tell them what they want from the child to satisfy their parental wishes. They don't meet the child and ask where the child is and how the child feels. Being told is the way of someone else's way, with little to no regard for the child's way. We have to fit into this tight box of the nuclear family.

If I went to my mother and said, "Someone said I was stupid at school," she would reply, "You're not stupid, you're smart, they were just teasing you."

This is not wrong. And yet, because the depth of understanding of how to truly communicate is not educated into humans, parents simply do the best they know, from how they know, from the way they were parented, or how it's shown on TV.

A way to have met me, seen me, heard me, listened to me from where I was and let me express my feelings safely, would have been to ask me how I feel about it, to allow me to speak about my hurt and pain, to allow me to get it out, and then have some love and some hugs. Then, the parent has allowed me to validate my own feelings and not simply told me how they think I should feel or think from their perspective.

It's subtle and a huge difference in how a child will feel later, and how they will operate life from then on. Once a child can express their feelings and not be told how others think they should feel, they can literally assist themselves in the healing and understanding of the circumstance. If not, they can just add this to the ten thousand wounds. I remember this well. I was always feeling like no one listened to me, they just told me what they thought. It was like I was stupid and invisible.

How do you feel?

How does it feel?

What do you feel about what happened?

These simple questions allow the child to feel they matter, they are important. And if they don't want to talk, you just express that you're here for them if they want to speak. No telling, no pressure.

CHAPTER 6

Curriculum

Now we are ready for the school of life. This is setting us up for the future, for our own personal lessons, teachers, and curriculum. We will now, in real life, move to small schools and learn to perform to get gold stars (the gold star syndrome), which adds to our now programed and conditioned self to seek out external validation, acceptance, approval, and love. The reward system concretizes and creates more need for the external as we continue to beg outwardly to feel good inside, to feel loved, and to feel safe.

In a tribe and community, we would simply all assist each other to keep each other, to love each other, and feed each other. We don't need to seek external validation for safety. We don't have to perform. There is no pressure to be how two people want us to be, or any other confined established system of chasing rewards.

So now we have created a bag of feelings of unworthiness, unloved, unsafe, undeserving, undervalued, and not good enough, all by ourselves. We did this. We interpret others' dysfunction, their behaviors, their play of their blindness, trauma, hurt and pain, and we create these beliefs about ourselves.

We are now also always on alert and under pressure to be sure we are being how others want. That's a stress that perpetuates and dysregulates our nervous system.

From varying degrees, the labels of unloved and not good enough are the perceptions we hold within us that now starts to form who we believe we are. The child's interpretations create its self-perceptions, which create beliefs about themselves, which then form a deep unconscious subconscious software program of the self, which holds all our feelings and thoughts about us.

This will be the lens we see through, the way we see others, life, and the world.

As the little child thinks, its conscious mind, from its beliefs, it seeds the subconscious with its thoughts about itself and life. We then create a constant loop of thoughts and words and feelings to keep life exactly as we make believe it to be. How magical we are. I will go into this later.

We are constantly, unknowingly, creating our reality.

Up to the age of seven, this continues like hypnosis. If our parents fight, or break up, or are drunk or loud, or are abrasive, or absent, or emotionally unavailable, immature, or aggressive, or violent, or not emotionally intelligent, and are absent in time and space—which is normal—we simply keep reinforcing our beliefs about ourselves from our thoughts about ourselves.

They are them, being themselves, in their own soup of blind and wounded unconsciousness. That's theirs. They are simply doing the best they can where they are. This has to be deeply understood.

We hold deep, hidden shame about not being good enough from us to us, and a big dollop of guilt and shame for not being able to be good enough for them. We feel inept, not good enough, stupid, bad, wrong, like no one cares or loves us. We are unsafe, seeking soothing, seeking external validation, and everything becomes either a soup of deep inner pain, or we try to compensate by being a good child, a smart child, a well-behaved child, or a good student. We have now become blind to our abandoned self, begging externally, and people pleasing to feel safe and loved. This is nowhere near our authentic self.

By varying degrees, we are now ready and fully loaded with ammunition for the school of life and all that has formed our nervous system, our mental neurological pathways, our unaware, unconscious, subconscious, and all the chemicals these jigsaw pieces release into the body that we are addicted to. We are an amazing addictive, habitually programmed and conditioned and constructed make-believe soup of us. And we are so used to this soup, this conditioning, these self-perceptions and limiting beliefs, that we are literally asleep at the subconscious wheel, ruled by them, and living in the past, and from our past. This is like software, malware, viruses, and all else that blurs the lenses of our perceptions of the operating systems of life.

The loaded gun of ammunition is ready for the triggers to trigger themselves from within us, with all that we need to see and work through.

Labels

The world likes to use labels of language. We have to, to a degree. We live in language. When this and that happened, when someone did something, or said something not loving, we created what they label as wounds, traumas, samskaras, our karma, our barriers of limiting beliefs inside us. We can also grow up and label it as abuse and toxic. We do this by how we interpreted circumstances and the behaviors of others from the youth and innocence of our child.

In the actuality of what is, what our parents did, they did what they did. It was. That is that. It was simply them being them. What was behind their cause, their actions or words, was them playing out their very own held-onto stuff, their very own old hurt and pain, their very own childhood interpretations and perceptions, or should I say, misinterpretations and misperceptions. And this heritage plays out, points, and projects outwardly and blames us, scorns us, shouts, frustrates at us, tells us, criticizes us, judges us, beats us, and even rapes us, and all else not of the soft and gentle loving of the unconditional. This was very similar to how their parents were to them. Hurt people hurt.

The labels toxic and abuse about others, are just that—labels. In actuality they describe effects and symptoms of causes, which are another person's hurt and pain, which they then play out without the ability not to. They don't know why they are being the way they are. And it's simply a mechanism born from hurt and pain from their own childhood.

Forgive them for they know not how they are, or why they are, and so, what they do.

This is very important to ingest and realize, regardless of the story of what happened. We then label them, label the story, label how we feel about them, how we feel about us, how they were and are, from our beliefs, and then live this way our whole life, until we see differently. We become a victim of our own beliefs, interpretations, and self-perceptions.

These are our stuck energies, like a scratched record, a loop of pain that replays itself again and again. Imagine all the ten thousand wounds of the past of words and tones interpreted and translated as we are not good enough. It's not actually what happened or what was said or done. We ourselves created the narratives of no good, even if it was screamed at us, or beaten into us, or worse.

Others unknowingly spewed their stuff onto us, and we took it very personally and made it our stuff. They did and said what they did and said. And WE felt hurt. We created the hurt. This very aspect of the actuality is the lens of perception of how we can now take full responsibility and accountability for what lives inside us.

They did what they did. They were how they were. How we were, what we felt, was our very own innocent creation.

So now we are full of stuck energy, stuck stories about ourselves, from ourselves, and about what we created about others. We feel lesser, no good, unworthy, unloved, and full of shame and guilt for simply not being able to be how others wanted us to be, and how they treated us, thousands of times over. As well as our own limiting barriers of beliefs, we also feel and think and hold negative thoughts and beliefs about others. We actually become a victim, and we blame, we create stories and narratives about them, from us, and replay them constantly believing them to be true.

We hold grudges, feel deep resentments, unforgiving, and sometimes hate and have deep rage. These are the pains from our deep unloved self, from inside us pointing outwardly. What is hidden underneath them is the hurt from not getting the love we wanted.

"Just love me!' is every child's inner scream and mantra that lives behind their hurt and pain. Just see me, meet me, hear me, listen to me, and love me for me. And these little pains all add up to become a dark shadow within, a constant that gets upset, disturbed, and literally dragged up every time our body remembers or feels something similar.

We call this being triggered. No one actually triggers us. Something happens outside us, and up comes the old energy, the stuck stuff from inside. It seems like the outside happening or another triggered us, the circumstance, what someone said or did, or didn't say or didn't do. But we are full of ammunition, full of the deep buried hurt and pain from our past, from our ten thousand wounds. We are the loaded gun, and we are the actual trigger that fires the ammunition of us outward.

We shoot the messenger who reflects this, and shows us to us, our stuck stuff, in the mirror of life. This is where we have to start to translate and navigate how to operate life from a whole new perception and understanding. Once I was blind, now I can see. We label others as abusive and toxic and say we have trauma. We say they are bad. These are labels we created, which are in fact effects and symptoms of how we interpreted other people's behaviors, born from their own hurt and pain. Now we live from our lens of a victim.

They don't know they are hurting and in pain, and we don't know they are hurting and in pain, and so we then create our own hurt and pain and blame them. It's not wrong, it just does nothing to free us from our hurt and beliefs.

The Mirror of the School of Life

We are now full of stuck stuff, feeling less than we did as a little baby, full of hurt, pain, and a bunch of barriers of limiting beliefs we built about ourselves as well as thoughts and feelings which can all fit into the nice bag called "My unloved not enough ness." In this bag is unworthiness, undeserving, unsafe, guilt, shame, bad, no good, stupid, wrong, no one loves me, unloved, and a few other less than loving beliefs we have collected, constructed, got stuck in, and informed within ourselves. We are an indoctrination of us. This is the forming of our very own subconscious, and this runs 96% of our life, apparently. No one did this to us but us. We interpreted others, we then created beliefs and perceptions about them and about ourselves, and then live through this lens of being and seeing. We see life and others through how we feel about us and see us. We have created holes in our essence and wholeness. We have conditioned our unconditional. We have darkened our enlightened bright child.

Up till the age of seven years old we are like hypnotic sponges. If a father or mother shouts something judgmental, belittling, with unloving tones, or to a degree of coaching, as in,

"You can do better than that."

"What good is that?"

"Who's going to like you for that when you grow up?"

it all seems normal. And it is. And yet those sentences can literally rule a child for the rest of their life. "You can do better than that," translates from a young child as, "I'm just not good enough, not smart enough, as I am. I'm not loved for how I am." It's so very subtle. We were talked to like this, so we believe we are like this.

I remember being shouted at and sulking many times thinking these thoughts about myself. I had parents, schoolteachers, and religious teachers tell me I needed to do better. I was teased and ridiculed by other students at school for not being academic. A teacher made me stand up and called me stupid in front of the class, with many other belittling words. I carried stupid and not good enough inside me much of my life. I had so much shame from being shouted at and ridiculed that I became a tough guy to cover it up and protect the pain and compensate so as not to feel it. That shut most people up, and it also got me expelled from numerous places of education. I hid from my pain and overcompensated by being a rebel, by being strong and wild. But hidden inside me was all the shame of not feeling good enough and stupid. That was how I felt in my deep subconscious. No one made me feel it. I interpreted the ways and words of others, of teachers, parents, and other students, and created my own beliefs about myself. We take everything to heart, and then we cover it up and close it to protect it from feeling hurt again. But this does not serve us too well. Now we are guarded, protective, and in a defensive place inside. We have hurt and pain sitting there, wanting to be loved.

And this is where the mirror of life comes into play in another way. We keep creating our life for us to see us, from our beliefs about ourselves. I felt stupid, no good, only bad and wrong. So, then I became tough to hide it. Then I got expelled from this place and that place. And guess what, I then felt stupid and bad and wrong. I created a life, sabotaged my life, from how I believed myself to be. It's like an invisible magic that simply does what I deeply believe about me. My unconscious subconscious runs the show. And my life shows me who I am, how I feel about me, deep inside.

My self-perceptions, my old beliefs about myself, then create an energetic resonance, that then creates projections, my deep feelings about myself, thoughts about myself, and words and actions and reactions which all match my beliefs and will then be seen in the reflection of the mirror of life.

I will unknowingly mess up my life to match my deep beliefs.

If I step backwards, follow my path, reverse engineer me, connect the dots, I come back to me, to see it was me who created how I feel. And I can then match this with much else of what happens in my life. From here, through the translation and navigation of the Map, I can see myself. Then I get to work on those hidden beliefs to dissolve them.

If I feel unworthy, I will make sure I stay in that worth. If I feel not good enough, as most of us feel, to varying degrees, I will sabotage my life to make sure this is my constant reflection. If I feel unsafe, like a lot of ladies of the patriarchy, I will demand more from my partner, leave my partner and blame them, or keep feeling like the world is an unsafe place. I might even attract some really dramatic circumstances to perpetuate how I feel about myself. Then, from my deep hidden beliefs, I blame the mirror, the other person, and call them names and label them, and remain a victim, caught in my unsafe self-perpetuating prison.

Much of the time we can also overcompensate and try to become enough, get more, find love and safety outside of us in many ways. And we can get and gain and attain someone and everything, but not to the inside hole we want to fill.

They say those deep in their victim mind will

be obvious targets for muggers. It's quite true. They hold themselves like victims, walk like victims, and give off an easy target vibe. That's not any different to how it works in the animal kingdom.

The mirror of the school of life is showing us where we closed our heart and fell into the barriers of beliefs of the mind and subconscious. The mirror will reflect us back to us. The mirror will trigger all the hurt and pain to be seen, to be healed. Others are simply showing us to us, being them. And we see others through the lens of us.

It is the feeling I feel that is the healing that needs to be healed.

In the past, whenever someone would say something and I couldn't understand, I would feel the feeling inside me, of the shame of feeling stupid. I didn't know what it was, and I would react, defend, even rage and attack, or shout back and put them down or maybe get angry and aggressive. How's this a mirror? The other people would simply be how they were and say what they said. Seemingly, "they upset me." Seemingly, "they made me feel like I felt." But that's only what it seems like inside me.

In the actuality of what is, they said something.

That's it. Then, I reacted. That's actually all that happened. That is the what is of life. But I reacted the same way I always did when folks would seemingly upset and touch and trigger my deep inner stuck stuff, my stupid wound.

It wasn't what they said or did. That's theirs, about them, from them.

Regardless of whatever anyone says, it's from them, about them, directed to me, but not actually about me. Even if they direct it at me, it's actually all about them, especially anything detrimental. Others see me through the lens of their own self-beliefs, their own self-perceptions about and from them, through their own stuck stuff, that they then push outwardly to me.

This is tricky, subtle, and stealthy.

Theirs is theirs and mine is mine.

This is the translation part.

Others' behavior seemingly causes anger, rage, reactions, raised voices, and even violence in people.

The words and actions of others mirror back to me what is stuck inside me, and a trigger inside me then gets pulled. That's what we all feel, much of the day about this and that, to varying degrees.

So inside me is the ammunition of my stuck stuff,

my unloved not good enough ness. And this very hurt and sensitive stuck stuff does not want to be in there. But I don't know this about myself.

Normally I just react when the trigger gets pulled, I pull it, and shoot my ammunition, say something in defense or attack with words, as well as feel unloved, unworthy, or not good enough.

"Who are you calling stupid?" I would shout. See, there's the clue. The mirror reflected back to me that I feel stupid and have shame about it stuck inside me. If I had no shame of my stupid wound, what they said would have no effect, no reflecting capabilities to show me my stuck stuff, and I would have no reaction to react from. I only snap and react from the ammunition inside me of my stuck stuff. And the reaction is the child inside me protecting me from feeling my pain of the old shame. This does nothing to heal me of my old sticky stuff. Nope, it just deflects from it, and protects it, keeps it from being known and felt and healed. When I was a very small child, I didn't have this wound inside me, created by me, about me. So, there is a me that is alive and well and not wounded, who has no stuck stuff, and no feelings of being stupid.

The old metaphor of this, told many times, is this: I can squeeze an orange and always get orange juice. I can't get anything else. When we are squeezed, when the school of life mirrors me to me, whatever is in me oozes out. If I don't have it in me, it's not going to be felt. I am full of my unloved not good enough ness. That's what gets triggered from inside me, and I spew it outwardly.

We all have our own unique curriculum, our schoolwork, to work on. Some ooze their deep beliefs of feeling stupid, some don't. Some ooze their deep beliefs of feeling unsafe to varying degrees more than others. The bag of beliefs oozes out all over our life and others.

The feelings I feel are the healings I get to heal.

The outside is mirroring me back to me, for me to see, for me to feel the pain, for me to sit with it, be with it, move through it, and for me to heal it by giving it this space to be held and seen. No parent did this for me, they just shouted or berated me, scorned me, and left it at that. I was left with my pain which I then kept hold of and added to my bag of unloved not good enough.

I'm not stupid, far from it. But it was an old

belief and self-perception I created about me. And life would continue showing this to me, and I would keep getting upset. I would be upset because I simply had not learned the lesson to heal the pain of the belief I ran from and reacted from. Life was showing me how to learn and heal, and I just blamed life and others.

All our upsets and disturbances are the lessons to learn from our stuck stuff that is triggered. The outside has nothing to do but show us to us.

They say we will always be presented with the lessons until we fully learn and heal.

A sentence I learned at my college of spiritual psychology sums it all up: It's not the issue that's the issue; it's the issue I have about the issue.

The outside happens. How I am about it, inside me, is what it's actually about. That's what I get to see about me, from me. It's not the outside.

Once I was blind, now I can see. We are unconditional beings who got conditioned, and then created our unloved not good enough ness. And when the pain gets triggered, we fling it back at life and others because it feels like they did it to us. No, they show us what's inside. They are our teachers and mirrors.

The lessons are healing these deep wounds of self-inflicted childhood beliefs.

The map, the operating manual to life, the translation and navigation, is to see this, know this, and to become practiced and consciously aware about it, moment to moment. Normally, before I went on my journey, I wouldn't be aware and would just react without knowing this of myself. Now I'm virtually always aware that the mirror of the school of life is showing me something stuck inside me. It's not the outside world or others. They are my teachers in the school of life, showing me the lessons I get to learn and get to heal from. The outside is showing me how to unload the ammunition, empty the gun of me, dissolve the past stuck stuff. Nothing is actually anything but the past being revealed, again and again, and then reacting its bad act into the same of the same. There is no change or healing and growth here.

CHAPTER 7

Reacting

Nowadays, when I get triggered, I mostly get to find my calm and not react, not defend or attack from my old stuff, my old hurt and pain and shame that's hidden inside me. Going into the immediate, deeper, slower breathing is a must in order not to fall unaware, and not to let the old protective and reactive self take over. I must find the space within me to see this. The feeling to react is so strong, so seemingly normal, that it seems incredibly painful not to react. That is the smart of my old ego self. It's trying to protect me from feeling the pain and hurt of my old stuck stuff. How very sweet of me. Seems kind of logical and sensible. But then, if I react, I keep all the stuff stuck, protect it, deflect from it, and do what is known and project from it, point outwardly from my inside, without any healing, or growth, or learning. I defend against, or attack, or simply judge and criticize back those who said what they said or did what they did. Or instead of an external reaction, I have an internal one. I just wallow in my not good enough ness, my unloved self, my stupid wound, feeling stupid, and I feed it more of the same feelings and thoughts.

That's the opposite of the school of life, not reacting, being with the pain, learning, healing, elevating, and evolving into a greater conscious awareness.

It's learning the translation and navigation of what's happening, and not reacting from my wounded and hurt unloved self that becomes the practice of how to operate my experience in a whole new way. I literally start to see through a different lens of perception. Life is a constant moment to moment classroom full of lessons and teachers. Grist for the mill, as Ram Dass said. Everyone is assisting me to see me, showing me to me, for me to see myself. How utterly kind of them. This is why, when I get triggered, I thank my teachers, regardless of the seeming circumstances.

Thank you, other car driver who cut me off, who has their own obvious stuck stuff, for showing me not to get angry, not be upset, as I always did, and just allow it to be what it was. It happened. He's moved on. How am I with me?

I can continue to repeat my old reactions and stay the same as always, or I can change how I am. Can I now breathe and not be that old me who feels disrespected by the other driver, feels shame of being belittled by his forceful driving? No, the driver did not disrespect me, they did what they did. I felt ignored, disrespected, shamed from my old stuff. WOW! They were just being them. Me, I was just being my old software playing out the same reactions of my old act of pain and shame.

Yup, we are operating in the past and from the past again and again and again.

If I get angry, impatient, frustrated, worried, anxious, resentful, jealous, or feel let down, it can all be worked on, seen as my deeper hidden old stuff and turned into peace instead of feeding the normal same old same reactions. This is a constant of being aware of myself.

Conscious awareness is the gift I give myself for being unconscious and unaware.

Others are operating from where they are. They speak and do, as they do from their stuff, as we do from our stuff. As with our parents, we must see everyone as doing their best where they are without knowing the map or the operating systems. Everyone is where they are. That's it.

Remember, you are learning how to see this new way, and most have no idea how to see this. This is also the mirror showing us how to find one of the greatest lessons and gifts to ourselves, the compassion we shall now nurture and practice. Forgive them for they know not how they operate. Nasty and hurtful words come from the deep pain of hurt inside. They say hurt people hurt. If the mirror hurts you, it's your stuff inside, your old hurt and pain, that's coming up to be presented for healing.

Other people's words are their own sticky stuff, their old hurt and pains, that are pointing outwardly, projecting at you to protect their pain and not face their pain. This is what our knee-jerk reactions are.

Our relationships, family, and love partners are full of triggers and projections. They are the greatest vehicle of healing and growth in life, but most have zero idea. I will get to this.

Turn your judgments into lovements!

The Only Way Is Through

So, here's the way of the map.

Someone says something. My wound, my stuck stuff, feels it, gets triggered from inside, and a strong feeling tries to overtake me, as well as a narrative in my head that seemingly matches with the outside circumstance. I want to point, snap, and react. This time I'm aware of it, I'm not falling into the trigger, I'm able to watch it. This time I'm ready, I'm in my conscious awareness. I feel the pain of my old shame, of the stupid, but I don't try to protect it. I feel it and know it's not a truth, know it's an old story, the past repeating itself, presenting itself to be seen and healed. I detach from it as I watch it and feel it fully. I breathe deeply and slowly. This can all happen in literally a split second. I don't react, I don't attach to it and feed it, I watch it, I keep sitting in it. I shine the light of my awareness onto it and into the darkness of my old self, my old story, my old unresolved wounds, my stuck stuff. Even if I don't know, I can't translate the wound, find the label, the narrative of the past, the shame of the stupid, no good, bad, wrong, unloved, unworthiness, I can still just sit in it, with it, feel it, and move through it. The pain of shame does not like to be felt. And much shame is behind the wounds of the bag of the unloved not good enough ness. This can seemingly be excruciating. It's actually simply the protection of the pain trying ever so hard not to have it felt and faced. It's a protective mechanism. We don't need to protect our heart anymore. In fact, we want to open it.

Sitting in the pain, and with it, and through it, is not something we have ever done. So, it will seem like a fight to do so. Who wants to feel the pain when you can point it at others, soothe, or feel unworthy and wallow and hide in the wallowing?

Our very resistance to feeling the pain keeps the pain and keeps us away from the pain. The pain keeps itself by not being seen and not being felt. The wounded child is still protecting itself, well after the fact. Another way to see it is that the pain is actually trying to show itself. It's screaming to finally be loved, to be accepted, to be healed. And this facing the pain is how I move through it to the other side and rise.

If I feel anything inside me, it's a message for me to look inside and be with the feeling, to be aware and watch it, not become lost in it and react from it. This is a presented opportunity in the school of life for me not to deflect and protect and blame, point fingers and project from my wound, but to move into it, face it, move through it, and out the other side with compassion and love.

This is a whole new way of operating the human experience. The feeling I feel is the healing I get to heal. It's a huge, heroic, and courageous thing to face our pain, sit in the feeling and move through it, again and again and again. This is not easy by any means because we have lived our whole life in the unaware habit of reacting, protecting, and projecting. So, we have to know this is a new practice, a new process, a new operating system. It's simply going to take great awareness, courageous and determination. That's the hero. Of course, if we are under physical threat, our natural fight or flight comes into action. This is not to be ignored as an old conditioned emotional trigger. This is our survival nature. Distinguishing the two is what we have to do. They can feel exactly the same.

This way of seeing and being is how we can constantly keep healing the past in the present, the old stuck stuff. This creates a practice of moment-to-moment awareness. All that upsets and disturbs us is an opportunity to meet it and face it and move through it. The normal way of our reactions is attached to a whole system that is connected and addicted to this way. Our nervous system is used to the reactions and protections. The neurological pathways are set in the narratives of defense and attack and blame. The unconscious subconscious barriers of our beliefs are where the pain and hurt are stored and getting triggered from. And all these release chemicals in our body that we have become addicted to. We literally have a force of self that is inhabited to react, deflect, protect, and then project.

These are all autopilot default settings of repeating the past, keeping it the same, and hiding the hurt and pain from being healed. This is why most people resist the work, stay in their victim mentality, don't face themselves, and don't take this heroic responsibility of moving into and through the pain. It literally means we have to keep dying to our old reactive self and face our pain constantly and not blame others or life. To do this and be in communication, in conversation, is where we have to navigate with conscious awareness and gentle, passive, responses. These are a practice in themselves. Once we take the charge out of the old reaction with our awareness, we can learn to operate at the same time. It's a whole new operating language of life. It will feel like trying to juggle for the first time.

Here are some conscious responses. Or a way to stop the reactions with a language break to assist.

I understand your perspective and hear what you're saying.

I would appreciate if we could communicate a little more gently.

I'm just a little triggered and might need a moment.

I value your opinion and respect and understand where you are coming from.

Is it OK if I express something to you?

Learning to have a nonjudgmental, non-defensive and non-passive-aggressive reaction is a new art of communication.

Being Triggered

What is actually being triggered is the bag of many things in the not good enough ness of our hidden subconscious being. We always feel, think, and then react within a split second from this place and space. This is what requires the new awareness, a new operating system. Whatever gets triggered gets felt in that instant, and it's imperative to become acutely aware of ourselves and not allow the tsunami of emotions and thoughts to override our awareness, create a narrative, and point, react, project, defend, or attack. We have operated our whole lives thinking the outside in, thinking the outside triggers us. The outside is a mirror showing us our triggers to our ammunition and what is under them. We have lived thinking and believing that we get upset and disturbed by the outside world and others.

Whatever is happening inside, it's not actually about the outside. The outside is literally showing us to us, for us to see, for us to feel, for us to move through, and for us to heal. This is taking full and utter responsibility. This means being able to respond with awareness and not react from the place and space of a wound and being a victim to others and circumstances. It is you who is your issue, you who is creating the problem, you who hurts, and you who feels. Ouch. No more pointing fingers at the outside.

The victim thinks the outside world is hurting them, upsetting them, insulting them, causing the emotions to emote and the thoughts to think. This is a whole new perception of life. The mind and body are so habitually addicted to reacting.

We have been translating the language of our mind and body quite blindly for thousands if not millions of years.

We are in essence unconditional beings who became riddled with conditions, wounds, traumas, and samskaras, our so-called labeled karmas. And this then creates our blindness, our schoolwork to work through in the school of life.

Most of our lives we have lived with very different perceptions of these understandings to knowing the Map. I know I have. And yet, my two-decade journey of my study and inner work has led me to a whole different way of being, seeing, and living within myself and my experience of my life.

I have fumbled, stumbled, reacted to, and defended my pain, my shame, many times. Even the man they labeled Christ, which was just a name for his consciousness, apparently lost his temper and turned the tables over on the moneylenders at the temple.

Don't beat yourself up. Don't berate you and belittle you. Don't be tough on you. Because that in itself is the effects of the parenting put onto you as a kid just repeating itself by you, from you to you. And it's another clever way our ego keeps us feeding itself, to keep itself a victim. That is the guilt and shame of all of us who had to perform to get validation. And here we are again beating us up, feeling not good enough. This is the beauty of the school of life. Even for beating ourselves up, we get to practice self-compassion. I'm OK with being here. Being here is perfect. I can allow this to be how it is.

The Map will always give you the next opportunity to use it, to take you inside to see what else requires working on. It's an endless constant of potential possibilities to keep healing the ten thousand wounds or keep protecting them.

We are always doing our best at any given moment in that given moment. And that has to be accepted, for our own sticky stuck stuff as well as for everyone else's journey through life. Where we are in our practice and journey is where we are.

Each time we get triggered by the seeming outside, we do the work. And there is also the same for the inside stuff that arises from within us, without external stimulus. Inside us is a self-critic, self-judge, our belittling, berating thoughts and words that all belong to our bag of unloved not good enough ness, our hurt child. These too have to be seen as old stories, old feelings, old barriers of beliefs we hold against us to keep us in a loop of our pain and hurt. We literally keep cementing who we think and believe we are.

I say we either cement our karma or cremate our karma. To me, karma is our being, our beliefs, our thoughts, feelings, actions, inactions, reactions, and words. We either keep poisoning ourselves with their very disease and remain in our victim or we face ourselves to heal ourselves and become our hero. We either keep soothing our pain or moving through our pain. We either hide and escape, protect and project from our pain, or we keep facing ourselves again and again. We either seek to get exterior validation and instant gratification to soothe and stay in the same or constantly bring ourselves back to our truth and inner worth by moving through the feeling and healing.

CHAPTER 8

Exterior Validation

We are all addicts of exterior validation. From a young child we had to be how others wanted us to be, to do as they wanted us to do, to feel safe, accepted, approved of, loved and validated. Before language, we were, within ourselves, authentic, pure, of our essence, true to our being, joyful, fulfilled, whole, complete, secure, safe, worthy, and loved within us, from us. We were loved for us, for how we were. Then, as we grew, we realized we had to be a certain way, behave a certain way, do certain things to get loved, and feel safe and validated. Tones and language were put onto us in many ways. It's a nuclear family thing.

So, we became what others wanted, for them. What does this actually mean? We neglected who we were, how we were, as we were, for us, we forsake our truth, we abandon our essential authentic self, our unconditional being, to become what others wished, for them, for us to feel safe, to survive. We literally forget about us, to do what others want, become what others want us to be. Now we have an abandoned unloved and not good enough self inside us. This is a survival aspect.

We then become actors, performers, maneuvering our way to fit in, to be good children, to feel safe. A cookie for this, a praise for that, and the reward system becomes part of our makeup, our conditioning and programming. They label this intermittent reinforcement. We get scraps of validation and love in between being told no, be quiet, don't do that, behave, stop that, do as you're told, punishments, shouts, put-downs, criticisms, judgments, blames and complaints, physical attacks, etc., and added pressures about how we are simply not performing the way others want and wish. We become performers, an acted character. WE abandon ourselves to become what others want to feel validated by others.

The gold star syndrome at small school has us in comparisons of others, which has us adding more need for exterior validation. I got a gold star. I'm loved, validated. Yeah! I shall tell my parents who will also give me value and love. But then little Sally gets four gold stars, and now I feel less within myself, and a need to get more from my not good enough ness. I'm now deep in the comparison and competition and the hypnosis of a brilliant blindness of trying and needing to be good enough, feel good enough.

Peer pressure, parental pressure, teacher pressure, systems of pressure to perform, and the greatest programming of all, that utterly hypnotizes my little child, the media machine of images and what's acceptable, what's the way to be, and narratives that perpetuate this undervalued state spew all around me.

We constantly subject ourselves to suggestions on a screen. And it's all selling the same show and tell and show and sell. Now I have to look a certain way and be a certain way to feel worthy, accepted and validated. And if I can't keep up, I feel unworthy.

The amount of information, suggestions, pressure, and conditionings to perform are enough to make a young child feel unsafe and wreck their nervous systems. It's like a hypnotic spell. And that's what this has done. To bring us to a feeling of enough, to feel safe, secure, worthy, valued, and loved, just for being us, is a hell of a magic trick as we constantly seek the drug of exterior validation. We are so blinded by trying, and needing, and wanting, and seeking, and hoping, to get our validation, that we keep perpetuating our self-inflicted self-critic inside that we aren't good enough and unloved. This is the cause of much human disease.

The unloved not good enough ness either wallows in itself, tries to find soothing, in distractions, sedations, stimulations, or any other escape, or it overcompensates to try to become more, get more, seem to be more, and show more. Look mummy and daddy, I did good! Validate me, love me, approve of me, accept me!

The last thing any child does is become loved and enough from within, by itself, with no care for the world of exterior validations and instant gratifications. The last thing a child does is feel secure enough to simply be themselves without a care of what others think. This is a rare child who simply sits in a Zen state, watching the rest of the hamsters on a wheel, racing rats.

The wallowing not good enough ness can range from a lackluster victim, always complaining about everyone and everything, blaming the outside, to a dropout, a drug taker, and someone who gave up and lives on the street. At the very end of this scale of the unloved not good enough ness is suicide.

And the crazy thing is, none of it is a truth, but a story we keep feeding to ourselves and believing and living with.

The soothing of our unloved not good enough ness is rampant and normal. We soothe with untold simple escapes. Be it sugar, weed, wine, booze, sex, porn, Netflix, social media scrolling, shopping, dating apps, getting married, and doing anything we can not to be with our deep unloved pain of not good enough ness. We are in a perpetual hide and seek. We have never ever learned to be with our abandoned unloved self and feel it all. To do this is the most foreign thing. Even as a kid, if you think about it, when we felt alone with ourselves, we were mostly being told off, sent to our room, or given the silent treatment. How painful was that? Why would we willingly wish to return to being with ourselves?

Even finding a partner, a relationship is the biggest soothing for most people and their unloved self. They seek their exterior validation, their safety, security, their worthiness in the exterior fixes of another. This is seemingly normal, and how humans have operated and navigated from their unloved blindness. And this usually causes much of its cause and effect.

The relationship is the greatest mirror of our inner poverty that seeks exterior validation. This will be explained later.

Overcompensation for external validation is simply how we all mostly live, to a degree. Some will excel at school, at sports, be the best they can to people please others and parents, become a high achiever, be driven to succeed, become famous, as well as be of service to others to feel acceptance, approved, loved, and validated. Much of our lives is driven by a deep unconscious need to get external validation from our invalid unloved not good enough ness. Unfortunately, the outside can never be enough. So many miserable marriages. So much scarcity in the wealthy. So much insecurity in the famous. We live in an outside-in world, when in fact we need to clear all the barriers of limiting beliefs of the bag of unloved not good enough ness inside to feel of any true value.

One extremely famous actor of the olden days, Sir Laurence Olivier, when asked why he got into acting, said,

"Look at me, look at me, look at me!"

This was an obvious statement of the unconscious subconscious belief of lack that needed and wanted to be seen, to be validated. This is the overcompensation of many in life.

We always come back to us, where we are inside us, where we were before we got gained and attained. We try to change the feeling inside from the outside. This is simply how humans are programmed and have operated for eons.

If I feel unloved and not good enough, seeking love and more outside of me, I can't ever become loved and more inside.

I will then just blame and complain about the outside and others from the triggered pain of my unloved not good enough ness. This is literally what most humans do.

CHAPTER 9

Inner Child Work
Self-Parenting

My journey is no different to everyone else's. I was parented. I misinterpreted their stuck stuff, their dysfunction, their unknown trauma and wounds that they then unknowingly put onto me, that they played out. Then, I created my beliefs about them and about myself. These are my own barriers of beliefs I created that closed and protected my heart from any more pain. I did this to me.

I worked with two incredible teachers for three years on the inner child as well as worked for two years with facilitating and being facilitated in a college for spiritual psychology. The process is simple and yet not. We have, if we can imagine, a little version of us inside us. And this little version of us is still holding onto all its beliefs, protecting its pain, and trying not to get hurt again. Unfortunately, this keeps us inside their protection mechanisms, the barriers of beliefs we have about ourselves, and beliefs we hold against others. We have inside us a deep unloved, unsafe, unworthy self, our abandoned child, we keep abandoning.

When I was at my college, everyone brought with them a picture of themselves at three years old. We formed two circles, an inner and an outer one. Every 25 seconds a bell would chime, and the inner circle would move to the next person in the outer circle. We all held our photo on printed paper at our chest levels. We had all worked for two years facilitating and sharing openly and vulnerably with each other. And here we were, after all our sticky stuff had been shared, seeing our little versions of each other from another lifetime ago.

To say I cried the whole circle was an understatement. To witness the authentic little faces of my classmates, and look into their real adult eyes, was astounding to see the journey of life, the wounds and traumas, the pains and darkness all dropped away as we all shared tears of joy. We were all the same. We were all such sweet, wonderful children. There is another child inside of us, the healed child. The child before they decided to carry the bag of unloved not good enough ness through life.

We are these two children.

When working with one of my great teachers, he would ask me about my circumstances regarding a breakup, and then ask me to shut my eyes. He would ask me to answer him without hesitation from the little boy inside me, how he would feel. Every time he would ask me a question, my little boy inside would speak without fail about his hurt. My teacher was a real talent at asking the right questions to bring it back to me, not to make a story, not to blame and point fingers but to describe how I felt about my life circumstances now, in the present time, about the breakup, but as a child.

How does he feel?

I always cried and always spoke of the fact that I believed no one loved me. This was a very deep core belief and barrier I had built my whole life. From this, much was seen, unraveled, and continued to spill its can of beans, now freshly opened. The amazement of my own inquiry from then onward brought up so many narratives I had pushed aside and buried long ago. And even to this day new stuff presents itself. I was full of shame for many reasons. My mother was harsh, physical, verbal, and terrifying. I wanted to die at a very young age. I hid in dark places. I feared love. It hurt me. My brothers teased me for being the youngest, and I simply felt unloved and no good, just bad and wrong. Add this to my belief that I was stupid, and I had a great bag of unloved not good enough ness to work with. I was brutally and violently beaten by cousins and one brother. I was always told I was too young because I was the youngest. That is translated by a child as I'm not good enough for being young. That just piled onto all my other beliefs. Add to this the bitter and angry divorce of my parents from three years old onward, and all their spite and bile and hate, and I simply didn't want to live.

My mother did the best she could being single with three boys for a few years, but I remember being scolded and shouted at loudly and aggressively with many strong sentences that I took to heart, and so I closed it to protect it. I got chassed and beaten with a wooden spoon. This was trauma again and again and again. No child should be terrified of their mother or father.

Now I had collected a ton of karma, of schoolwork for the school of life. I constantly pushed love away due to my fear I would get hurt again. I closed my heart to protect my heart. My smart inner child protected me. But this old wound was unhealed, and the protection kept me from opening up in relationships. The mechanisms I used to keep me safe from pain, and the belief that love was dangerous and painful, would simply have me sabotage my dating world and create a life of being rejected and cause me pain and the feeling of not feeling loved again. I had created a mirror from my beliefs. I was not being loved because I deeply felt unloved.

So I did all my work at college as well as four years kicking and screaming in my first conscious relationship with a smart-ass lady, had a big break up, then worked with my numerous masters and teachers who taught me how to do inner child work. I memorized my photo of my little child and used that imagined image to talk to, to speak to, to ask questions when the pain felt bad, or the hurt felt bad, or I simply felt upset or lonely. And it was always incredible what his voice said. I'm stupid, no one loves me, I'm bad, I just want to die, no one cares. Why can't I just be me?

My job was to listen to him and be there like the most loving soft and gentle parent, something I never really had as a child.

I asked him what he needed. I spoke softly and told him I was here for him, that we're going to do this together. He would soften, smile, and find a happier feeling. This work is astounding, transformational, and incredibly sensitive, healing work. This work is moment to moment.

We must be soft, patient, and gentle with our inner child. We must not be how our parents were with us. We must meet the child where they are and not tell them or scold them. We see them in all their pain. Boy, have me and my little boy cried again and again. I made songs for us that were the antithesis of all my barriers of beliefs, and I still sing them with him. They lift me. It's truly magical to be this parent for myself. I love the song. I sing it many times daily, especially in the mornings.

I think everyone should sing this to themselves every evening before bed and in the morning, or when we need a lift. I think children should also sing this. You can tailor it to your own special needs and wants. To me it covered all my limiting beliefs.

I'm brilliant and I'm greatness
I'm brilliant and I'm greatness
I'm brilliant and I'm greatness
And I'm loved, loved, loved.

I'm the bestest and the greatest
The bestest and the greatest
The bestest and the greatest
And I'm love, love, loved.

I'm brilliant and I'm greatness
I'm the bestest of the best
I'm love and wealthy, healthy
And I am a great success

I'm brilliant and I'm greatness
I'm the bestest of the best
I'm love and wealthy healthy
And I am a great success

I sing it over and over and love it and won't ever stop.

I also sing into the mirror every morning another tune to give me love.

I love me
I love me
I love me
I do,
I love me
I love me
I love me
It's true.

Repeat as many times as possible, any time.

I'm always there for my little child inside, as soon as I feel some downward feeling, asking him, being there for him, loving him, creating space for him. Meeting ourselves where we are, seeing ourselves, and listening to our child is not how many of us were raised. This is our constant healing.

I am still there for my little boy, still singing with him, and he is now much closer to the little boy who was simply all love and joy before the barriers of beliefs were built.

When I'm triggered, I can also use this tool to inquire how he feels inside about what upsets me. And it's always revealing. And then I'm there, being there, meeting him, loving him, bringing to him all he asks for. And it simply heals a little more every time.

The school of life has a lifetime of lessons that takes time to learn, to practice translating, and to come to healing with. And as we do these practices and processes, we alter ourselves, find that little bit more love, more safety, more worthiness, and we heal. And as we do this, as we change from inside, life starts to reflect different things back to us. As we heal, life reflects it. Our lenses of perceptions change from being a victim to taking full responsibility for our inner stuff.

All that is unhealed within us in life is mirrored back to us, triggered within us, and is being presented as our lessons to heal in the school of life.

The unworthiness, underserving, unsafe, unloved, not good enough ness all cause their effect of showing us to us in life. Why is my life like this?

It is bringing you teachers and lessons to show you what you need to see, what you need to face, to feel, to move through and heal. We will only live from these not good enough places inside if we don't use the Map.

Regardless of our overcompensating, we always come back to our not good enough ness. Regardless of the partner or marriage, we will always have our unloved and unsafe sticky stuff from our childhood reflected back to us. And that is what we point fingers at and blame, and project at our partner, or life.

Being this parent we never had, is the love we always wanted. And this is the work of always being there to be there for us.

This work is a constant, a moment to moment. If not, if we are not there to be there for our abandonment, we simply stay abandoned, and life will keep triggering it for us to be with it, face it, feel it, and heal.

CHAPTER 10

Parents

Parents were parented by parents who were parented by parents who had no fucking idea what to do. A fireman, policeman, doctor, lawyer, accountant, nurse, ambulance driver, soldier, therapist, and all else, all have to be qualified. What are the qualifications to be a parent? You must have private parts.

So now we have two humans, your parents, who have names, who were not mum and dad for much of their lives, and like you, had to cope with life without any understanding of the map, of the operating systems, and so did the best they could without any real actual life education. They were raised by people who did the same. The patriarchy and nuclear family and each individual's own sticky stuff of life were then carried into their whole new life of being an uneducated parent. Before they start, they are already dysfunctional and full of unknown hurt and pain. This we must fully see and understand. Many of our parents had a very tough time.

Now they get to try to raise a child, or two, or three, with no understanding whatsoever. Oh, yes, the human mother got to practice with a plastic doll and push it around in a tiny push chair and feed it fake tea in a dollhouse. That's an education for real life for sure. And then they had a lifetime of the fiction of the TV and movies that showed them that dysfunction was normality.

These two wounded and blind humans, with a whole bunch of their own stuff, who had lives they were trying to cope with, undertook the added untrained and unmapped task of bringing you into this world and raising children out of the nature and nurture of community.

With virtually no support, constant financial struggles, their own unknown mental and emotional baggage, they then bring a child into the world. And this is when all the behaviors and pains of their past, hidden deep inside them, start to be triggered to come out and play out, all over you and your siblings.

Your parents live in you, like it or not. The way they related to each other, how they related to you, and how you believed they related to you and how you felt about them, all affect your life, how you feel about you, relate to yourself, and especially how you relate in your relationships. They simply did what they did, with the tools they had, and that was that.

Repeat information

How we felt, how we interpreted our childhood, was done by us. Even if our parents seriously abused us, beat us and screamed at us, or demanded we do more work, or be better, it was actually us who interpreted their behaviors from a blind and ignorant innocence, and then created the self-perceptions and beliefs we held inside us. We created the bag of unloved not good enough ness and then held and made judgments against them. We did this.

We interpreted their stuff and then we created our own stuff. This is imperative to understand. Because the mirror of life is going to reflect this to us constantly in many ways, and especially in relationships. We formed who we are from us, by us, to us, by trying to interpret our parents' own blind baggage and barriers of beliefs and behaviors. Their inability to know how to operate in the patriarchy and nuclear family is simply a normality for 99.9% of humans. It all seems like normal operating systems.

Full steam ahead.

Every word, action, reaction, tone, and physicality were computed by our innocence, from a point of reference from the unconditional of the breast, to then do the best we could in computing and down-loading our operating systems into our secret hidden and unknown subconscious. Unworthiness, shame, guilt, underserving, unsafe, stupid, wrong, bad, no good, not good enough, and much else, all build our deep unloved self from inside us. Simple sentences like,

"Don't you know how to listen?"

"You can do better than that."

"Are you stupid?"

"Don't you know how to think?"

"What kind of grades are these?"

"You will never amount to anything if you behave like that."

"I won't tell you again."

"You drive me crazy."

These are a tiny fraction of seemingly harmless sentences that cause their effect.

And there were many more, in varying tones and varying degrees of unloving, stern, and authoritative forces, that are all interpreted by our innocent minds. This is the ten thousand wounds. We just did the best we could from where we were. And they did the best they could in trying to be the best they could, from where they were, with no operating manual, no education, and a bag of hand-me-down sticky stuff spewing all over the place in their words and actions.

Their pain of their childhood spilled into our childhood and became our pain. And we blame them, belittle ourselves, and live from these perceptions which then rule our whole lives.

If you truly ingested what I just wrote, regardless of the story you hold against your parents and the beliefs you hold within you, you must now find the deep compassion and understanding and the forgiveness this brings for them and for you, and especially your little child inside you who held all these hurts and pains of barriers and beliefs.

We start with an innocent open heart. Then, word by word, action by action, scream by scream, hit by hit, and more, we keep closing our heart and begin to protect it from being hurt again. We form mechanisms and barriers. We resent, hate, get angry, hide, sulk, and feel lonely, like no one cares. We pretend we are OK in our walled-in self-protections. But we secretly pine just to be loved for us, for who we are. We are stuck in this stew of self, of the unloved not good enough ness.

To do the work to dissolve the walls and mechanisms is courageous. It means facing what we didn't want to face. It means taking the protection away and feeling all the stuck pain we didn't want to feel. This brought for me a huge amount of crying, wailing, and dying to the protective, wounded child within. He served me well for then, but then served me far too long causing all sorts of problems and self-sabotage in life and relationships.

Our parents did what they did. It was how it was. They played out their blind and wounded play. They had no idea how to cope. We can't alter what was. We just wanted them to be how we wanted, for us. They were also very hurt and full of pain to varying degrees.

When I found out about my father's childhood, all I judged him for and held against him dissolved. I suddenly saw the pattern of his protecting his heart, and all else. It does not excuse his behavior. It simply brings deep compassion for the little boy behind it. The same for my mother. And believe me, my father had some issues he put on everyone in our family.

I was the only one toward the end of his life who kept in contact after no one else was talking to him. A sad old man, in a home, riddled with dementia, with no one. When I found this compassion, found this greater understanding, I dissolved my judgments and all that lived around them. That in itself was healing.

I decided to go see my father. My family thought I was mad. He had done some things to us all that were quite awful. Yet, for me, it was time to go give him a hug and tell him I loved him. Believe me, if I told you the details of why I stopped talking to him for six years, you would think I was mad.

He was a mafia of a man. His ego was bigger than his 1970s Cadillac cars he drove around London. He bragged about hurting people and was always macho and full of bravado. He was a strong, handsome rogue. He was charming, for sure, but he had a very dark, sordid, and violent side. And each of us in my family experienced our own story of him.

When I went to visit him, the man I knew was gone. The dementia had robbed him of his bravado, his wounded ego. He was stripped down to his truth. When he realized it was me, the first thing he said was, "Why did you come to see me? I've done terrible things."

My answer?

"I came to tell you I love you and give you a hug." We talked. He was now a gentle innocent little boy of him. I showed him pictures of my brothers' kids he had never seen or met, his grandchildren. Tears rolled down his face. I kept telling him I loved him. And he kept telling it to me. Then, when I had to leave, he got out of his bed, all skinny and weak, and we hugged and cried and whispered we loved each other again and again, like never before. This was the greatest moment of my life for healing. This can actually happen inside us, from us, to us, without the parent. I had already forgiven him and found compassion and love before I even made the journey to see him.

The same thing was done with my mother, but she was no longer alive. I found the compassion and understanding that she did the best she could. She also had a story buried inside her she didn't know had affected her. She loved me so very much. And I had to see this, know this, and grieve the loss of love from all my life of resenting her for not being how I wanted. I wailed and cried and wailed and cried for my mum like a sweet little boy. And after a good year of this work, on and off, in private and in public, I was greeted with her in an astounding vivid dream that I know was not a dream. And we hugged and hugged and hugged with a lifetime of love. And boy, did I cry in my bed with insane joy. And it was my prize for letting go of all I had held against her. It was the opening of my closed and protected heart. It changed my whole life. I softened and opened and felt more love than ever before.

All she had done was unknowingly play out her own pain. And I blamed her, resented her, and was angry at her. And I get it now. That anger and all else was the little boy who just wanted to be loved.

Forgive them for they know not what they do. Please, do this. It's the most beautiful thing you can do for you, for the rest of your life. I have tears just writing this.

When you can come to truly embody this truth, it can liberate you from so much pain and hurt you carry. And it is our very own disease we keep alive by not doing so. We don't have to be with living parents who are dysfunctional. We can simply process this without contact. Forgiveness and compassion are a gift to us. And when we do this work and take our judgments out, our living parents will actually become more bearable. And they will seem to be more acceptable.

Wayne Dyer once said, "When we change the way we see things, the things we see will change."

Once we forgive them and release that weight, enlighten ourselves of the past, we get to then face our own part in what we innocently did to us. We created the beliefs and stories of our unloved not good enough ness. This we have to also find compassion for, and also forgive ourselves for holding onto them. And it is these stories and beliefs about us that the mirror of life always shows us. These are our triggers and pains we don't want to face.

My last big breakup was all about not being able

to heal my deep mother wounds. I knew nothing of what I know now. I had zero idea of why and what and how to navigate and translate my way. Everything I have learned and become since that breakup, all I have written here, and all I am inside me now, is because of what I had to face and how I had to heal.

As the realization of the compassion set in, as I healed my parental wounds and all the shame, I began to release blocked energy. I cried and wailed and cried and wailed. It was like shedding skin after skin, again and again, dying to my past self.

And from this, grief came up, not only for my mother's death, but from my whole life. And when you live with unforgiving and all else, you miss out on the compassion and love that lives behind it. I had spent a life not living in the love that was always there.

As we heal the past in the present, we change our future. As we forgive and find compassion, we are left with more space for working with the judgments we made against us, our barriers of limiting beliefs that have restricted us our whole lives.

Mixed with what was going on with my abandonment issues now being faced about my mother and my breakup, which was actually all about my mother and not my ex, it was excruciating and beautiful all at the same time. Still to this day, I will release with tears of joy more pain and hurt and find more love as my heart continues to open more and more.

I tell people, this is a process, not an event. If I took you to the ultimate of the unconditional within you, in an instant, if you healed in a moment, you would either explode, end up in a lunatic asylum, or not be able to cope with life in such a new and evolved state. Evolution is a journey. And this book is about moving from the victim's story to the hero's glory. We literally continually keep rescuing our victim of self again and again, moment to moment, whenever we fall into our darkness or get triggered.

So now you can see we grow up with this bag of unloved not good enough ness and beliefs about ourselves that rule every aspect. These labeled wounds, traumas, misinterpretations, misperceptions, which are our life school curriculum, or our karma, all sit inside us. Deep inside our subconscious self are stories we believe to be true about our parents and stories about ourselves. We now live a make-believe life. And these are our backdrop. We have been feeding ourselves these victim narratives since childhood. We constantly feel all the unloved, not good enough ness. We berate, belittle, judge, criticize, put down, doubt, fear, protect, defend, attack, and project our ideas and beliefs of who and how we think we are onto the movie of our life. The actor has their wounded character playing out their own unknown drama. How does this play a part in the map and mirror of life? These unloved not good enough nesses of our self-perceptions create how we operate, how we function, how we think, feel, talk, act, and react. We will see the reflection of our inner stuff mirrored back to us by others and life. We feel ourselves in our reactions, our triggered stuff, our feelings. The world and others mirror us to us, constantly. We either don't know this of ourselves and blame and bitch and moan and complain, in our victim, or we know this of thyself, and become more aware, and do the work, and feel the feelings and do the healing, and become the hero.

This emotional bag of sticky stuff just wants to be healed. That's what 99% of all the disturbance and upset is about. A baby is unconditional, you could say a mild Zen. But they soon become a bag of unloved, not good enough ness. So we learn to practice and process our way back by seeing all the opportunities being presented to us, as we feel them and don't point fingers, project, blame, and complain from them, move through them, and dissolve them bit by bit, again and again.

Normal life, in our blind uneducated state, our insanity of humanity, does all it can not to face our stuff. Our unloved not good enough ness can be a victim of itself, overcompensate, or constantly seek soothing. And this is a constant of needing and trying from our inner unworthiness. This is our disease. And these deep pains we don't face will always be triggered and mirrored back to us by circumstances and another person in our love relationships and all else.

CHAPTER 11

Relationships

R omance, marriage, and happy ever after. We have all been raised by these ideas, these programs, these narratives. Now add up everything I have written, and you will see and understand that we are full of a whole bunch of unloved not good enough ness and sticky stuck stuff. And due to this baggage of our barriers of beliefs of our unloved self, our abandonment, the indoctrination of romance, marriage, and happy ever after, we operate thinking that someone else is the answer, that some exterior validation will love our deep unloved self. We have been chasing cookies, gold stars, grades, praise, exterior validation, and love our whole life. And we chase from this inner place of our deep neglected and unloved self. This unloved self seeks someone else to love our unloved parts and soothe the pains.

When I find them, the ONE, they will ease me, soothe me, rescue me, save me, complete me, be the love of my life, make me feel better inside me, and assist me in basically not feeling so unloved, unsafe, insecure, unworthy, and not good enough. FINALLY. Thank God.

We operate from our blind and wounded abandoned self, which has been reinforced by narratives of fantasy and fiction in the media our whole life. Happy ever after, the prince and princess, the hero, the damsel in distress, and a lifetime of the beliefs of the fantasy that the future will all be OK, the pain will be taken away.

No one can heal what is inside us. No one can do that but us. No one, nothing, and nowhere can heal inside us. This is the bitch of the reality that bites.

So we have a fantasy and fiction hypnotized into our psyche since childhood. Hallmark, Disney, romantic comedies, and all else of books and the media narrate the same narratives. All is written by writers who operate in the same indoctrination, who have the same baggage, who think and feel the same as we do about romance, marriage, and love. The stage is literally set. We grow up, fueled and full of unloved pain, then hit puberty, and then all the notions of our fantasies and fictions, mixed with wounds and hormones, come flooding in.

Here is an example.

The girl I liked speaks to my twelve-year-old self, and I'm intoxicated, on cloud nine, ten, and eleven. I instantly fall blindly into my hypnotized and intoxicated fantasy, dreaming of our wedding and eating ice cream together forever. Yes, men do this stuff too, they just won't admit it. I'm in love. I'm silly dreaming in each moment, and nothing seems to be wrong with the world. I'm loved. I'm loved, screams my abandoned unloved child of not good enough ness inside. I'm of value to someone. How amazing this feeling feels. I now do all I can to be the best me, to try to get her to love me again, love me more, and be my girl. She is also doing the same inner dance. We have two intoxicated preteens falling into what they label as love. How many of us have done this again and again? And how many of us have felt the deep intoxication of exterior validation and the pain of breakups and what we call heartache?

Because we operate with so much unknown, invisible, unloved not good enough ness, the exterior validation and attention floods us with feel-good chemicals. This is the intoxication of what we label as the honeymoon period. We literally operate drunk. All the pain of a lifetime of our unloved inside stuff is now soothed by exterior validation and the delusion of the potential happy ever after. Operating from these places is normality. And this is why so many problems arise.

The education of the navigation and translation of the communications of relations is mostly mute and void in 98% of humans. We have lived in romantic notions of fictions for centuries.

First, we have to understand this aspect of love. We are operating blind and drunk, addicted to exterior validation to get a high, a fix, to feel soothed of the abandonment pain of our unloved loneliness.

Second, we are fueled by a lifetime of programming and conditioning that someone else will make the pain of our loneliness go away.

Third, we have been hypnotized into a fantasy of what marriage is about.

Marriage

Marriage was first created as an arrangement to secure genetic diversity and peace between neighboring tribes or nearby communities. There was always an equal transaction of cows and sheep or chickens or whatever to make everyone happy. You get free milk, we get free eggs, and we support each other and bond, and our children aren't mad, insane inbreds. Perfect.

Love, and what we label as romance, had fuck all to do with it. And till death do us part was written into the original contract when humans lived to about 34 years old. We all mostly lived in communities, and women were literally treated like cattle till up to 100 years ago. Rape and beating your wife were quite normal and legal in the history of humans.

Romance and love were rarely what marriage was about. Our modern happy ever after is just a fictional idea, first presented in books, then plays, and then in a massively media-hyped, scripted fantasy created by storytelling for a recent and modern era.

It's an amazing added and updated twist on an old-age business nuptial. And we have run with it and turned it into the ceremony of vast business and statistical failure ever since.

56% of marriages fail. That leaves 44% that don't. That's already a less than half-assed bet to success. Out of those 44%, 75% are actually miserable. That equates to a roughly 11% chance of a true happy ever after and an 89% chance of misery and failure. These were statistics from the 1980s. I don't think it has improved.

Folks stay because they fear to be alone. They stay out of habit. They stay because they fear the stigma of divorce. They stay for the kids and for financial reasons. They stay because they simply have very little love for themselves to actually leave, let go, and face themselves.

A long-term marriage is no sign of deep love and intimacy. In fact, it's mostly the opposite. It's a monotony of complacency, over compromise, resentments, and unhappiness with zero real, actual, true, deeper intimacy, growth, healing, or a higher union of love. This is the harsh truth folks don't like to see or hear. It's kind of like a bad habit.

That's the bitch and truth of what is. And it's simply the cause of the effect of most people not knowing themselves, or life, and how to operate what is actually going on. Being married for 40 years and watching TV every night and having a few drinks is not intimacy. It's a habit of numb avoidance. You win a prize for simply putting up with someone for the duration. This is simply an attachment and dependance for many. A familiar tone of autopilot, same old same.

There is no education of the navigation and translation of, no true deeper communications. And this will cause a constant of triggers and reactions that seem like normality.

The Mirror of Another

Relationships are the greatest vehicle for healing and growth in the school of life. That's actually what is going on. This is their very design. Yup. The deeper orchestration is mostly unknown to the average love-smitten, abandoned, intoxicated, indoctrinated human. Your parental stuff from your childhood and your partners is joining in an invisible, magical, magnetic attraction for you both to heal.

You attract the healing you need to do, to liberate you from your deep, abandoned, and unloved self. Many meet the partner with the familiar energy of the parent you least got on with, or got the least love from, who you thus wanted more love from. Your nervous system wants the same dysfunction.

The abandoned, wounded, unloved stuff inside us, which our nervous system is totally in tune with, familiar with, and ironically feels safe with, even if it was utterly unsafe, seeks out someone who is familiar to the dysfunction of the way you were raised. Why would a very smart system designed to keep us safe want to be with something unknown, and so seemingly potentially dangerous?

Even if we had abusive caregivers, it's what our deep unconscious system knows to do. It's like an unknown magnet. You're just like my dad. You're just like my mum. It's called divine orchestration. Our nervous system is far smarter than our conscious, thinking, smitten beast and wounded ego that fools in love, drunken and intoxicated.

I say we meet and attract the match of the lack of our self-love. We meet the match that reflects what we need to see, feel, and heal. They will show us to us, our underbelly, trigger our pain, push our buttons, and reflect back to us what we have to resolve and dissolve.

Trigger City

We meet. Our unloved not good enough ess becomes totally intoxicated into the exterior validation of another. Now we fall into a drunken play of two actors doing their very best to get love, feel loved, and soothe their deep, unloved sticky stuff. We usually sense what they call red flags, but we are so drunk we push them aside to feel the feeling of finally feeling full, loved, and in love. The pain of our deep, unloved loneliness, which we can't stand to be with, feels long gone as we start the drunken journey of falling into relationships. How astounding. The stage is set. The actors are ready for their upcoming dramas.

Now, I'm going to move past all the lovey marshmallow stuff, the labeled honeymoon. That's just the biological drugs playing their part, the chemicals flooding our body and brain to make us feel like life is all perfect, our abandonment is healed. And it seemingly seems like it is.

Exit the Honeymoon

When the intoxication thins, the projections begin.

As the honeymoon melts and the fiction fades,

reality bites, and the fantasy finds normality and trigger city begins its magic.

It's kind of like going to a bar, getting totally drunk, going home with another drunk person, having wild, crazy, kinky sex, and then waking up sober, thinking what the fuck, who the hell is this?

But this is like two years of drunkenness, not one night. The degree to which we are unloved, abandoned, and have deep mummy and daddy issues, is the depths of intoxication we fool into. What goes up must come down. Even as I write this, I know it's going to piss folks off. I'm a killjoy of all the fantasy, a whole life of wishing and hoping, of expectations and delusions. That's good. Being triggered means there is stuff inside you to face.

See, I'm your teacher showing you to you. It's not what I write or say, it's what you feel about it inside you. The issue you have is not me, not my words, it's the deeper issue inside that's being upset by my words. I'm a mirror in this relationship of you and me. And this is what now starts to happen as we sober up into our reality of relationships.

Believe me, I'm not against love. I'm a big, soppy, crying fool for romantic movies. But due to my inability to hold a relationship, and the rage and pain I felt, the time became apparent, with all this inner work I was involved in, to spend several years delving deeply into the subject of relationships and love.

We have to know thyself to heal. And we have to truly know what and why to see this of the self.

So the other person is now going to trigger you and push those lovely buttons of your deep, hidden, unloved stuff. And as I've expressed, the trigger and its ammunition all come from inside you, from your past. They are now your mirror, your greatest teacher, in the school of life. And your lessons are to translate and navigate what the trigger and feelings are all about, move into them and through them, and not point and blame and criticize from them. Unfortunately, this is rarely known, educated, and practiced.

We normally operate from our blind and wounded self. Someone says, or does, or doesn't say, or doesn't do something and we feel hurt and react. We point fingers, complain, criticize, and blame them for upsetting us.

"You make me feel like . . ."

"When you say or do that, it makes me feel like this."

We react and they react, and we play a power play of I'm right and you're wrong. Then, maybe someone might concede, give in, make the peace, hide their deeper resentments, just to make happy. Or there is a genuine apology and love is restored. This is the same play our parents played, the intermittent reinforcement. It's how we know how to relate.

The truth is no one makes you feel anything. WHAT?

Your feelings happen because your sticky stuck stuff gets touched, triggered from within you, and you don't want to face its pain. You feel. That's what happens in you, with you, from you, and about you. That's what is actually happening. This is like a whole new language in life. We think other people hurt our feelings. I mean, do they actually climb inside and mess with our feeling parts?

So you react and are now protecting your deep, unloved pain, deflecting from it, and pointing fingers and projecting it at others.

This is the actuality of what is going on.

"You touched my deep painful parts I don't want to face or feel or look at and heal, and so you did this, you hurt me, you are the bad guy, and I'm the victim."

No, they are your reflection in the mirror of the school of life, and your greatest teacher showing you to you. And you don't like what you see, and especially don't like how you feel. The truth hurts, as they say.

Well, what hurts is not the circumstance, not the issue, not the other person, not what they say and do, but the deep stuff you hold against one of your parents, or the beliefs you hold against yourself that are now triggered and being presented to be healed. This is an actual opportunity. What? They pushed my buttons, they upset me, they did this! That's the victim. That heals nothing and keeps the pain hidden and unhealed.

No one does anything to us but show us to us.

So what's the solution to the reactions and projections? Non-reaction.

This is called full responsibility and full accountability. The ability to respond and not react. The ability to own your own shit and not fling it.

This is like swimming upstream, against the current of your normal protective victim behaviors and mechanisms. You normally use your reactions as a protection. You never face your pain. You always defend and attack. Or you simply sink and sulk into your unloved and unworthy self. Victor Frankl, a wise man who was in the concentration camps of Nazi Germany, wrote one sentence about this:

"Between stimulus and response there is a space. In that space is our power to choose our response. In our response lies our growth and freedom. "

To be non-reactive we must understand the mechanisms in place of reactions. The hurt and pain of the unloved aspects, the sticky stuff, do not want to be faced. They are what get triggered. We then go into automatic default reaction to protect the pain, deflect from it, and point fingers at the others we think touched our pain.

FREEZE.

PAUSE.

Hold your horses.

Let's go in slow motion.

I'm triggered.

Something inside me feels something.

Something inside me thinks a thought that wants to send words out to the other person to say something to defend my inner feelings of hurt and pain.

Wait.

Now go slower than slow motion.

Deep and slow breaths begin.

I best not react the normal act I always react.

I must allow this feeling to be seen and felt.

I shall now step back inside me, detach from the story of the outside, focus inside, see it, and watch it, and at the same time take a deeper breath knowing I am not my feelings or the story in my head.

It's now not controlling me, I'm in control of me and it.

I see it, feel its pain, and allow myself to move into it, with it, and through it.

I am not attached to the pain or become the blame and story of its projections.

I sit in it and with it and all the way through it until it burns like a flame and turns to ashes.

I do not give in to the very strong and real addiction and defensive mechanisms to the reactions of the past.

This all happens in an instant. This is a practice of breaking a habit of a lifetime. Not facing the pain is like an addiction to our old operating systems to react and protect and blame.

Whatever anyone says or does that's not loving is

about them from them. That's their own stuff pointing outwardly, their own hurt and pain protecting and then projecting. Theirs is theirs. Mine is mine.

How we feel, what happens inside us, is all our own stuff, our own hurt and pain that seems to be about what they say or do.

Being able to see this, not to react, and to take full responsibility is not the normal way we operate. So it will seem very clunky and abnormal and like a force is trying to get us to snap and react.

It's all pretty much all our childhood stuff. Let's just bag it into the unloved not good enough ness. And that's what gets upset, disturbed, and triggered. The wounds, the traumas, the samskaras, our karmic curriculum, are not healed and presenting themselves to be so.

It's like another person jabs their finger into our old wound and we have to react quickly to stop it from hurting. Usually, we try to hurt back, snap back, react, or put down, and passively-aggressively, defensively, send out another sentence. I call this projection tennis. Two wounded people flinging their sticky stuck stuff at each other, protecting their sticky stuck stuff, and blaming each other. The ego really loves to be right. There is no growth or healing in that, just more of the same old same old same power play at play. That's normal relationships. We have been raised by those who were raised by a heritage of not knowing the map of how to translate and navigate life. And so we all learned and all normalized our inability to live without a map. We are now relating like our parents. And as I've said we have a media narrating the old way of operating in cartoons, movies and TV showing us the normalization of reaction and blaming and projecting. We are being shown utter dysfunction as normality.

So we meet and attract, and also match, someone who is going to reflect back to us our unloved self, our bag of not good enough ness. At first, it all seems dreamy. As the dreamy drug thins, the schoolwork, our homework, begins. We get triggered. We react. We blame and complain and bitch and criticize and basically keep doing this on and off until we normalize it, become familiar with it, and just live in it, with all the hidden resentments and anger and unhealed hurt and pain that constantly get triggered again and again.

Or we educate ourselves, like you are now, and learn how to navigate and translate what's actually going on. If you are reading this book and you are in a relationship, it would be very wise for you both to read it and both be on the same page. This is imperative. You will finish this book and be seeing things through a new lens of perception. And no one wants to be told or taught by their partner how to relate. That's like living with your parents all over again. That itself is you trying to change someone from your own not good enough ness.

"You need to be how I want you to be, so I can feel safe and happy."

Trying to make someone change to keep us feeling safe is our childhood unsafe stuff we need to work on. And the pressure to try to get someone to love us more, make us feel safe, is a nonacceptance of where they are and who they are, which is rejection. Who wants to love anyone who rejects them?

We are pulling the curtain back like Toto in *The Wizard of Oz* to see the false of the noise and light show and fireworks of frictions and fictions of relationships.

An example.

Someone once said to me, long after a breakup, that I made them feel unsafe by my decision to stop communicating. We were not dating anymore, just dear friends. I had kept breaking off contact when they started dating another person. We had already agreed if it was not healthy, I should not stay in contact. I was not ready to handle them with another person because I had stuff coming up, I had to work on. I had not healed yet from my old stuff. My feelings were all about me, and I expressed that it was not healthy for me to stay in contact. I had to break free, break contact, and figure out why I was reacting so strongly.

In time I did the deep dive, worked through a lot of excruciating pain of shame about not being good enough, as well as learned to love myself more and stop people pleasing.

She had now moved on two times since our breakup. And yet I was like a puppy dog, always there to please and be the support in between each man. That's a wounded place to behave from. That was me people pleasing mummy to cling to some external form of validation.

Her feelings of feeling unsafe were hers, from her unsafe feelings triggered inside from her own unresolved stuff from childhood. I was just a mirror for her, as she was for me.

If I had no wound to work on, I would never have clung on like a lovesick, unloved, wounded little boy with mummy issues. I would have just moved on and shut that door, with love.

And after my deep inner work, crying and wailing and working with my inner child, I looked back and saw very clearly how I was operating and seeing through the lens of my abandonment pain.

If she had no wound, no sticky stuff, she would have a deep compassion for and understanding of where I was, send love, and leave the door open without the statement of "That makes me feel unsafe."

We both showed each other our stuff. I couldn't deal with mine, and she was showing me hers. I walked away to face my deep shame and pain of feeling that no one loved me.

I can't make you feel anything.

No one makes us feel. We feel hurt and pain from our old, deep, hidden stuff. The unconditional lens of perception sees life from the greatest understanding of compassion and love. The conditioned and wounded lens of perception always shows itself in our hurt feelings. We are being shown us to us through the mirror of life, through circumstances and especially others, and those we love.

Hurt feelings are simply a signpost to what we have to work on, look at, face, feel, move through, and heal. And this is one of the hardest things to do, to avoid pointing fingers and projecting and blaming, but rather to see that it is mostly our own unworthy, unsafe, unloved stuck stuff from our mummy or daddy wounds.

The anger, hate, and resentments many feel about others is the hurt and pain of the abandonment wound of their childhood shame being presented, that they had never faced, but covered up with dating or marriage. And it's so utterly painful, they don't know what it is or how to face it, and so they turn it around into emotional ammunition and point it toward those who have mirrored it back to them. It's beyond genius and normal human understanding.

Another example.

When a man feels his shame triggered, his little boy who feels stupid, not good enough, wrong, bad, or unloved will react to cover the pain of his shame. He will speak in a higher pitch and louder tone and be passive-aggressive to varying degrees. He will snap and react quickly and not face himself, his hurt.

And this is the cause of much violence from men to women. Their shame is so painful that they get a rush of chemicals to their brain called abandonment rage, and they literally go blind with anger and rage. I am sure it also happens with women. They are not devoid of rage. I myself have experienced this from the other side of the fence as well as my own side.

Whatever is said with a snap reaction, or a sarcastic put-down is protecting wounds, deflecting from it, and then blaming, pointing fingers, and projecting from it. This is the opposite of what is actually required from the man, which is a deep vulnerability to open up and show his pain and old shame.

How he should function from a clearer lens of perception is he feels the feeling, the thoughts start to try to narrate an attack or defense, but he stops it before he reacts. He breathes, comforts his inner child, little boy, and sits in the pain of the shame and moves through it.

Communicating is a key to the alchemy of pain.

His response might be, "I'm feeling triggered. I need a moment, please. I understand how you feel, and I appreciate you expressing it to me. If you would like to sit down and talk about this, I would love to know if you are ready and OK to do so."

There is an astounding book, and I'm not too keen on its title, but its contents will trigger most people for sure. I've been humbled to study its teaching for several years.

The book is *Getting the Love You Want*, written by Harville Hendrix and his wife Helen Lakelly.

This will truly enlighten you about how to translate and navigate relationships. This book has been around since the 1980s, and it's been a huge bestseller. And right now, this education is very much becoming the new understanding of relating.

We are entering into a new place in human conscious evolution and the development and understanding of how to operate life. The above-mentioned book was well before its time and is now perfect for where we are, in our time. I always recommend this book. I always say that both you and your partner have to read it and operate from it, with dedication.

If you two are not on the same page, it's futile.

When we meet each other where the other person is, not from where we are, we can both truly meet each other.

Our parents didn't meet us, so we learnt this osmosis way of relating. We see others from us, from how we want, for what we want from them, so we can feel safe, loved, and happy, and it is usually through the lenses of our abandonment, our unloved sticky stuff. This is simply how our parents related to each other and to us. You be how we want, do as we want, behave how we say, and we will love you. We are like clones playing the same play of a heritage of blindness.

I'm trying to make everything as easy and simple to understand without complicating it or over-articulating. I repeat myself to make sure the messages get through. Another person triggers our stuff. We trigger their stuff. We both fling our stuff at each other without seeing this, without translating this, without navigating this, and so without healing this.

In essence, we all simply want to go back to the breast, the womb. That initial imprint of life was so strong, and we never got the unconditional again, and we have been chasing it ever since.

The unconditional lives within us all. We simply created our barriers and blocks of beliefs that get in the way. For most people, dogs and babies, and baby animal videos, burst their hearts wide open

DAVID DAYAN FISHER

again, and all barriers drop. It's inside us, always. But the barriers soon go back up to protect us from any potential feelings of the hurt and pain from the past.

We will literally sabotage our relationships just so we don't have to face these deep wounded parts. We will push others away rather than face our unloved pain. The genius of our protections, blaming, finger-pointing, and projecting onto others makes every excuse and reason not to face ourselves.

This is the resistance to facing the pain. I was incredibly resistant a long time ago. The power of our trauma and wounds, their brilliant ego narratives and emotional protective forces are very convincing. Why would we want to be in this uncomfortable, painful relationship? It's not the relationship; it's our own wounded and blind relationship with ourselves. The logic of the ego is to run away from the pain. And that's how we stop ourselves from being open enough and vulnerable enough to face the pain, feel the pain, move through the pain, see it as our unloved shame and pain, and bring love to it by being this loving space for it, and to heal.

The wounded little girl and boy inside us sabotages life and relationships to make sure the old stuff about feeling unloved and unworthy is true. It's astounding. We make sure no one loves us by blaming others for not loving us enough. This is our own not enough, unsafe, unloved stuff blaming, projecting, and pointing fingers. It's so subtle and smart. But all we want is love, right? Yup, but we don't want to face the pain we have to face, to heal, to truly get to the love we deeply always wanted.

It is the pain we need to move through and heal that stands in the way of the love we already are.

We are full of love. We can feel love, and be in love, within, without anyone. This is not the same as being loved or getting love. Being loved is an external gesture that warms us, albeit temporarily. And getting love is the unloved parts of us that need and seek a Band-Aid for our abandonment issues, the unhealed, unloved not good enough ness. Once we ourselves are enough, then we are victorious. Not many of us have ever experienced a fully healed self. We operate blind and wounded, full of unloved stuff being triggered here, there, and everywhere, not knowing or seeing the healing work being presented. We blindly beg for some Band-Aid for our abandonment in another to soothe the pain we don't want to face by ourselves.

CHAPTER 12

Teacher in the Mirror

W e are either a victim of our unloved self, or we take full and utter responsibility and accountability and face ourselves, like the hero of the named hero's journey. The victim points fingers outwardly, at the mirror. The victim blames others for the feelings they feel inside. The victim is normalized over thousands of years of humans not having the map and knowing how to navigate and translate life. The victim is not wrong. In fact—and this is a tough one to understand—there is no wrong or right. There is no good or bad. Those are judgments coming from a lens of perception of what they metaphorically called blindness, in biblical terms. And even most religious people don't know of this deeper understanding.

Once I was blind, and now I can see. Hopefully,

after reading this book, your lenses of perceptions have shifted, been cleared, and you see slightly, mildly, or massively differently. You can see things you used to see as wrong, and now see them as someone operating without knowing what they are really, actually, doing, or saying. Each human is where they are, in their own wounds, their own constructed character, their own journey, believing in it, while being full of unloved not good enough ness, defensive mechanisms, and their protections and projections, playing them out on each other without knowing this.

Forgive them for they know not what they do.

I watch couples argue. It seems normal. I work with many privately and hear the same stories in everyone. And yet they don't know to see the operating translations and navigations. I see my own inner triggers that want to react and operate the old way, want to point fingers and project, and I course-correct and move through and rise above by using the navigations and translations of the map. I hear it in words all around me. "They did this, and they said that, and they do this, and they didn't do that."

They should have done this. And I'm upset because . . . Their issue they have about others is the issue.

I'm Upset Because

This was another great line from my college learnings.

Another great way of knowing about how to translate in relationships and life is this telltale sign that shows us we have to face our hidden inner stuck stuff.

"I'm upset because . . ."

This is speaking from something inside us, while pointing outside of us. We are pointing at the mirror. Life is showing us to us. This is the blame, moan, judge, criticize, and complain.

An example:

Someone decides at the last moment to cancel going out for the evening we had planned for weeks. They say they have to do something else with someone else. Not an emergency, just their decision to do so. I simply agree by text saying OK. Yet inside me a triggered feeling and narrative of my old self decides to start a victim story.

We had planned this, talked about this. It's rude. It's not how to treat people. Etc. etc. There is obvious hurt and upset inside me. I was raised by a mother who was very punctual, always on time, and she was always angry at others who let her down. I always made sure I was on time and never upset her or made her angry. I became the same for much of my life. I expected others to meet this standard. I would get deeply angry and upset and feel disrespected, as my mother did.

My father always said he would come and watch me play rugby, and I played and played, watching to see if he showed up. He never ever did. And every time I would play my very best, in the hope that I would turn around and he would be there, meeting me, validating me from the sidelines. My greatest teacher. He let me down, again and again. But did he? No, there is no actual letdown. I was simply reliant and dependent on him to validate my unloved aspects inside me. Damn. That's how slight and subtle this is. He was just being him. I was in judgment from my abandonment. I'm a victim, or I see from another level of perception. No child knows this, unfortunately. Maybe one day the map will be taught to children and a whole generation will grow up with a fraction of wounds from their upbringing.

I shall break down the actuality of what happened in this situation.

I made plans to go out.

The night before someone said they could not come.

That's it.

That's the what is of what is.

That, in itself is what happened.

That's the actuality of the circumstances.

Their reason was theirs.

How they were was all about them.

How I was, how I felt, the feelings it created, how I wanted to react, was all about my inner upset.

"I'm upset because . . ." So now I can either be a victim and blame them, get angry, project my upset, and cause friction, or I simply just accept what is and then do my work on what is inside me, what has come up to be presented as an opportunity to heal.

I could then simply have written and said please give me more time in cancelling next time and had no other emotional upset.

So I sit in the feeling. I don't attach or get caught in the narrative. Remember this is my teacher, a mirror to what's inside me. If there was no stuff in me, I would simply accept their way, their reason, and let it go. What was triggered in me was a deep hurt feeling of abandonment. I asked my little boy inside how he felt. He said, "I don't need anyone. I can do this on my own." Well, that was my way of not facing the feeling of feeling let down, not listened to, being constantly lied to as a kid by parents for constantly breaking promises they made. It was also my mother's pain I copied when others changed their minds or were late. It seems like the other person was rude. It seems like it. But what came up was a strong reaction inside me. And that was not just a mild letdown. I sat with it. I sat in it. I watched it. I did not allow the narrative to point from my victim and get angry with the person, or text them telling them they were rude. I then saw I was quite OK with them not coming for my own reasons, in truth to myself. I was actually looking for a way out because I wanted to stay in with my old and sick dog. Now I got to see my wound, sit with my little boy, and do some healing. The lesson might present itself again and again until I simply don't get triggered as much, or even at all.

So, the real deep upset was not what happened, but my old stuff. I sat in it some more and kept more dialogue with my inner child. They don't love me! This was the core of it. My ten thousand wounds as a little boy were activated, and I was being shown more healing. I saw this, I expressed gently to my inner child that this was an old story far from true. I gently told my inner child I loved him very much, I'm here with you. And eventually the upset faded and dissolved. This process can take a few days, a few hours, and eventually a few minutes to simply a second or two. We are all learning the process of a new operating system. Eventually, when I finally found love and compassion for my inner child and lost all the charge and anger toward the other person, they texted to come over for a visit. The subject was not an issue, and we continued our friendship without confrontation or upset.

Now, if this happens again, I will simply say that I would prefer not to have things cancelled last-minute. I don't wish to make a habit of this. My time is precious and valued, and I could have made other arrangements. I set my open and honest boundary; I establish my love for me, I don't people please in fear of not being loved. If it happens again, I simply express I won't be making plans again. I respect and actually love myself to the degree that no one can disrespect me.

Hurt Feelings

No one can actually hurt my feelings, insult me, or offend me. Think about the unconditional young child. Much of what offends and upsets us would have zero effect on them. For one, they have no narratives about themselves, no formed identity, no constructed ego, and so no ammunition that can be triggered. They are virtually free of the labeled wounds and traumas, they have no sticky stuck stuff, and have yet to make interpretations, perceptions, or beliefs about themselves or others that form the unloved bag of not good enough ness. They don't hold anything in their system other than an unconditioned perception. They have no disease.

Only the children will enter the kingdom.

Now, add to this child all the human conditionings and self-created and self-constructed ego identity, full of sensitive, stuck, sticky stuff of the bag of unloved not good enough ness, and it's a walking loaded gun full of ammunition waiting to be triggered. It's actually a perfected design to have the mirror of the school of life then reflect them back to them, to see themselves, face themselves, and move through themselves to heal themselves back to the unconditional child they were.

You can't go to school if you have no schoolwork. We get given our work in childhood for our adult to undo. It's kind of a sick joke. Why can't we just be enlightened and live our whole life that way? The human experience is a school. We forget our wisdom when born, and then have to become full of darkness to find the enlightening of life.

As the education of the Map and much else like it becomes more and more known, more and more children will be raised in a whole new way, and the whole of society, the writers of narratives in the media, will alter accordingly. We are pioneers of transforming ourselves and so each other and the collective.

Be the change you wish to see.

So, someone says what they say. We have established that anything not loving coming from someone is a pointing-outward projection of their own hurt, their own pain, and their own old blind operating systems.

Theirs is theirs.

But if theirs affects us, triggers us, offends us, upsets us, insults us, first we have to see honestly that we have allowed this to happen. Yup, we allowed their words to mirror back to us the hurt and pain that is waiting to be triggered. Which translates as theirs is theirs and mine is mine. And if theirs triggers the triggers in me, and I feel like reacting, defending, or attacking, or I feel upset, then I'm being shown what's mine, what's stuck in me, what's my issue about the outside issue. Thank you, teacher, in the mirror.

Usually, an aspect of your identity, or the old pain and hurt of your childhood you unknowingly identify with, that you are attached to, will cause hurt.

Words seemingly hurt you. I was raised in a Jewish family. It was my choice at one point in my life simply not to be, not hold, that identity. If you insult, slur, or get angry at Jewish people, or call me a foul name about being Jewish, I have zero ammunition or attachment or a need to defend or attack. It literally holds no hold within me, has zero trigger to anything stuck that I identify with. If you get upset by this, that's your identity being triggered. You see. I also know words are about another person's own projected pain and hurt. If you spew anger and hate, you are in pain. I can now have compassion for you and not feel hurt from you.

Instead of defending or attacking and reacting, I will say to you thank you very much. I do that to most who decide to throw angry words my way. It's a little cheeky. But I now mirror back to them who they are. I don't accept their hurt and pain. It usually ends right there. If you are of a color, or nation, or sports team, or political side, or any side divided so, you will mostly get triggered and upset by anyone's words seemingly against you or aggressively directed at you.

Words, what are they? Literally? They are letters, joined together, forming words, forming sentences, then spoken outwardly with intentions and tones. They come from a place and space inside someone, driven by their emotions, their thoughts, their interpretations, their own identifications, and their self-perceptions. Words are someone speaking from them, about them, to you. Yup. What you are hearing is someone mostly speaking about themselves. We are all talking through the lenses of our self-percep-tions. Which means, most people don't know they are full of stuck stuff, speaking from it, and think they are speaking about you. They get triggered and their stuff speaks. Then, if we have stuff, our stuff gets triggered, and we spew words from our stuff we don't know about. We are flinging our stuck stuff, our inner shit, at each other and not healing.

Forgive them for they know not what they do or say.

Know Thyself

For much of my life I did not know this of life, of myself, of others, of the map. I had serious amounts of ammunition, hurt and pain I would fling outwardly in words at others to deflect, protect, and project onto them. The power of the energy, the emotions of our reactions and triggers, is a force we mostly don't think of facing, and we usually give in and react.

It feels like a tsunami. A lifetime of reacting to triggers, to others, backed up by a deep unloved bag of not good enough ness and its hurt and pain, is mostly avoided. This is normality. Being in the pain, moving into it, and not reacting and not pointing fingers and narrating from it, is a rarity.

Some people don't become reactive outwardly; they literally shrink into their shell, restrict themselves, become submissive, and sit on their pain internally. This is just as damaging and unhealthy.

This Map work, inner work, is very confronting and courageous.

Coeur, the French word for heart, is what this is about. The journey from our head, our ego, our identity, its wounded and blind, unloved not good enough ness, back to our heart, back to the unconditional, is a choice we can make in every moment. We have spent a lifetime living in the past, recreating it in the present and continuing onwards into life.

CHAPTER 13

The Past, the Present, the Future

The Past

It was what it was. It happened. And it exists in the shadows of our unknown operating systems. We burp, hiccup, and rinse and repeat the past, acting out each knee-jerk, autopilot reaction. We literally run an old software program, a story, a belief system, of a once-upon-a-time, unloved, not good enough ness. We are a habit of, an addict of, a blind force that knows not of itself.

Our whole system wants to be how we know how to be, feel how to be, think how to be, speak how to be, and act and react how to be, built from a long time ago. We are actually living in the past, recreating it, unknowingly, moment to moment. Literally nothing we think or feel is new. Most don't face themselves their whole life. And there is nothing wrong in that. The Map is simply a way of literally altering and changing the past in the present.

The Present

The present is all there is. We fill it with the past and destroy it with the fear of the future. We drag our not good enough ness, our baggage, our weight, and our darkness into all our relationships and keep our barriers of beliefs make believing ourselves to be true, here and now, constantly. Our past unworthiness, unsafe, underserving, not good enough, stuck stuff, plays out in our very present moments in our unawareness.

But the present is the magic that can change the past and the future. If we use the Map, learn to navigate and translate each moment, practice this new process of operating life, life will constantly provide us with moments in the present to do the work, sit in the space of non-reaction, feel it all, and move through it all to dissolve the past and create a new future. The power of the present changes the past by not living in the victim narratives and by taking full responsibility to utilize the moments to change how we are. And when we keep changing how we are, we alter the past and its old influence on us, and so we alter our future.

Why drag the drama of then, the victim of then, into the future of when?

The Future

Today is yesterday's future. Yesterday was the future of the day before. We either drag the past into the present and then push it into our future, or we literally use each moment of the present to change our future by changing our past in every present moment.

Then became now. And now becomes when. Best to be using the map and constantly dissolving the past and creating a new future in the present.

The Human System

I am a body and a mind. My body from childhood has been growing, taking on information, creating self-perceptions from my interpretations, and living with beliefs about myself, with barriers and blocks of a bag full unloved not good enough ness.

Once, I was literally the space that all this went into. I was what is known as conscious awareness. My emotions, feelings, thoughts, words, actions, inactions, and reactions are all energetic aspects of my functioning, how I operate. This is my ego, my construct, my identity, my personality, my character.

Attached to these constructs are chemicals my body releases, neurological pathways that create how I think, the patterns of my mind I follow, and programs of behaviors and beliefs deep inside me, that we call our subconscious. Then, there is the ruler, the nervous system. This is where everything connects. It's like the engine room. How our nervous system is, is how much else follows, because all else feeds the nervous system so that it functions. This loop of our being is how we have been, how we stay, why we are why we are, and why we mostly don't change. We are a habit and addict of these systems that all run together to make believe who we think we are. We have informed, suggested, looped, ingested, digested, manifested, and metabolized ourselves into a self-creating self of who we think and believe ourselves to be.

And the mirror of life reflects this all back to us. How I am is why I am the way I am. And why I am the way I am always speaks itself into existence with my words about myself and life, and so creates more of the same. We formed our self-perceptions as a child. Then these barriers of beliefs, this bag of not good enough ness projects onto the screen of our movie, our life, and reflects back to us in the mirror of the school of life. Usually, if we have a blame or complaint, it can be traced back to how we feel about us. The whole system runs on the past. We live like an old software program, constantly feeding the system by not being aware of this repeating loop. We simply think we are who we think we are, operate how we believe we operate, and that's just who we are, without any self-inquiry. We are a cloned version of our own rinse and repeat system of self, playing the play we play, and have always played, keeping the farce alive, the system fed, and the whole body and mind constantly unaware of this fact of its act.

Unsafe and Inseucre

Last night, in my sleep, messages came through, as they do quite a lot, regarding what life's problems are about. Most of us from the patriarchy and nuclear family have created a perfected practiced barrier of beliefs that we are unsafe and not secure in life. Inside, we are virtually constantly in fight or flight mode. We were always trying to be how others wanted us to be for us to feel validated, loved, fed, and safely housed. In the community we had so much more support, so many more people around us all the time. That in itself created a safety net of sorts. Everyone was there for everyone, supported everyone, assisted everyone, and took the pressure off everyone because there was no actual pressure to perform. The nuclear family is mostly a very fragile and delicate dance of learning to operate life from. We utterly depend and rely on two people, if we are lucky. And that's already a stretch for them, while trying to earn a living, pay bills, and run a home and life in the modern world.

So, we are born, raised into constantly having to perform to what others wish, for them, to keep them happy, so we feel safe. That, on its own, without anything else, means we essentially feel unsafe and insecure about life. Now, from this, our mind makes up its own beliefs about itself, our system addicts itself, and we live insecure and unsafe, always seeking security and safety outside of us. Everyone is operating this way, talking this way, acting this play, and so we join in the play thinking it's all normal. It's a scrambled egg of constantly seeking outside of us to feel safe. This is fight or flight. Normally, when we were cavemen, or hunter gatherers, this way of being in our body and minds would mostly only happen when under attack from an animal. Now we have become an anxious, nervous, wreck, constantly trying to survive from a very young age.

This is our disease.

Perform for parents, for schools, for peers, to feel accepted, approved, validated, and safe, and then we become bombarded by comparisons and images on the media to look a certain way, behave a certain way, and have certain things.

We chase anything and everything to feel safe, feel good enough, feel secure, feel validated and loved from our bag of unloved, unsafe, not good enough ness, and its barriers of beliefs. And we can't ever find peace and rest inside because the outside can't heal the inside.

Our not good enough ness can never find enough outside itself, and so it's always feeling unsafe and not enough. Our parents couldn't bring this feeling of safe, loved, and enough ness; schools couldn't, and nothing else, no one else, and nowhere else can. We always come back to how we are inside us, unloved and not good enough. Damn it!

How Do We Become Safe and Secure?

There is no way to promise an actual safe and secure future of circumstances. Life itself is uncertain. Understanding this, and accepting this, is a huge start. And yet, in every moment of the present moment we can course-correct, use the map, and change our past patterns of neurosis and operating systems by being aware of our inner self, our insecurity and unsafe self, by using our awareness, and our insight. And the more we work on this, the greater we learn to practice, the more we alter our patterns. And the more we learn to alter our patterns, the greater our intuition becomes, the stronger our awareness becomes, and we continue to gain control over our past blindness and unconscious fears of feeling unsafe.

I call it my in-sight and in-tuition.

We have a chance to change every moment of every moment that we fall into a narrative in the mind and a feeling of fear in the body, of this or that, of doubt, or worry, or an insecure and unsafe feeling that starts to feed the old addictive machine its old patterns.

We literally have to be aware of whatever comes up within us that is a thought and feeling of unsafe and insecure. We see it, shine awareness onto it, breathe deeply and slowly, give ourselves a space, know it's our old self, old operating systems, and we then detach, don't tell a story, watch it, feel it, and move through it. I tell myself, "This is not true, it's an old story. I'm ok." I've got through this before and will get through this again. And now I simply keep my awareness on it with compassion for my old protective survival systems. This, like all else living with the Map, means a constant conscious awareness of what is happening within me. I have to be the watcher of my old self, or my old self will fool me.

Be it a flat tire, a person being late, someone not behaving as we wish, a sudden traffic jam, the washing machine crashing, the toilet not flushing, the dog getting sick, the engine warning light coming on, the boss putting pressure on us, our partner getting anxious, our children not behaving, etc.—life is always giving us so many ways to feel nervous, anxious, insecure, and unsafe. They are not actualities but rather our old self simply feeding itself its addiction to itself and all the systems that are addicted to operate in survival mode. It's very unhealthy. It is our constant restlessness, our unease, our anxiety, our worry, our fears, our self-deprecations, our frustrations, our impatience, which are our constant addictive dis ease. I tell you this as a fact: When we start to change, our whole body chemistry changes. We stop focusing on survival and bring back so much life force and energy for the body to return to its natural healed place.

Think about it: your whole life has lived in your unsafe, unloved, not good enough, and insecure mind and body. It can't take it. And eventually it screams with manifested disease and sickness and pains. This is now a science of the new medicine. It's out there. I recommend Bruce Lipton's book called *The Biology of Belief.* It is a game changer in educating the self on how our consciousness, our state of operating, effects our very biology.

Life is like the game snakes and ladders. When life's dice roll, when circumstances arise, we can either react, fall from grace, and slide down the snake of our normal reactions and emotional and mental patterns, or we can go to the space of non-reaction and breathe, knowing it's an old narrative, old way, old program, and move through it, elevate above it, and climb a ladder.

The addiction to our old self is unknown by most. The unsafe self literally wants to be unsafe. What? We will attract unsafe partners to feel secure in our familiar unsafe, create unsafe narratives about money, about our body, about our health, and speak words of our unsafe neurosis, worry, anxiety, and all else attached to our scripted ego's suffering not good enough ness. We are make believing life from our beliefs about us, creating more from these ways and words.

Abracadabra

In ancient Aramaic Hebrew this word meant "I create from my words." Our words speak of our life, and our life reflects these words. We are speaking life into itself by being how we are, and then spelling the spells of the words we speak.

What came first? The chicken or the egg?

Was it the life we created, or the words we spoke about the life we create? Was it our bag of beliefs of feeling unloved, unsafe, unworthy, and not good enough, or our life that feels unloved, unsafe, and not good enough?

We live in this loop of life until we know this of ourselves, see this of ourselves, and start to become aware of our words. And being aware of our words is an alteration of knowing what we say, what's being said, before we say it.

Do you think a man who always says, "I'm always unlucky," is ever lucky? Do you think a man who always says, "I'm always lucky," is always unlucky?

On a scientific level, we have the placebo effect of mind over matter. This is the mind thinking something is going to heal them when it is just a sugar pill. We think we will get better, and so this simple mental energetic cause has its effects. Every cell is listening to our mind and words and feelings. Our thoughts are the same as our words, as in our words come from the place of thought to process them and send them out. They resonate and create from inside out. Our beliefs, our self-perceptions, create our thoughts, which create our words.

The ancient texts all reflect his. Ask and you shall receive. I am that I am. So if I keep saying how I am about how I am, then I will always get more of the same. You see, how we are, our being, can only do one thing. We can only become that which we are. What? How I am being, how I am, becomes itself. We keep being the same, thinking the same, and speaking the same words about our life, from our deep beliefs about ourselves and life. Life and our words magically match. Abracadabra. Being becomes itself. The most powerful words are those that follow the two words of creation: I am or I'm. We speak of our scarcity, of our diseases and sickness, and believe it so, our victim, our struggles, how hard life is, how difficult it is. We believe our barriers of belief about us, our not good enough ness, and so create a life that mirrors them back to us. We literally create from our beliefs. We could even say we receive that which we believe. We drag the past into our present and keep creating from there onwards again and again. Nothing can actually change until we do.

No one has ever become that which they are not being.

Being becomes itself.

Here is another ancient quote: "Those who have, so shall it be given. And those who do not have, so shall it be taken from." This expresses that what we talk about, how we are, in our self-beliefs, our mindset, our feelings, our words, our transmitting frequencies into the quantum field of potential, is what we then get. If someone is living feeling scarcity, poverty, unworthiness, undeserving, not good enough, in their beliefs about them, they will use words to express this. And so we are now creating a loop of life. We feel and think and believe and receive confirmation in life that match the words we speak in the mirror of life. Those who have no doubt, have great faith, determination, and an enthused inspiration usually create the words that match this energy and then the life that mirrors and reflects.

They, whoever they are, say we are magical, energetic, manifesting beings. Well, this seems to add up to our words being the source of our creations. But the words are not the whole magic trick. As I said, reverse engineer the words of doubt and fear. Here is an example.

I'm really struggling right now. I'm worried about the rent. I can't stop thinking about what I'm going to do. Why can't I just get a break. I'm always just scraping by. I always just make it every month. I'm never going to get out of this mess.

These words come from thoughts and beliefs which also have a feeling driving them and matching them, which create words. It's not our circumstances that cause our feelings and thoughts, it's our beliefs and perceptions from inside us. It seems like it's the circumstance.

We feel not good enough from our childhood. We were raised in scarcity and so live in a poverty belief. We don't feel deserving and feel unworthy, and so we speak from these places. Our nervous system, subconscious programs, inner critic and judge, and our words that speak these beliefs, can only create from them. We can overcompensate but will always come back to our inner poverty.

This is why married people bitch at each other from their deep, unloved self. They project in words how unloved they feel by the other, their mirror, about their own deep, hidden beliefs about themselves.

We can get success and fame and still blame and moan and complain about the world from our beliefs within, our poverty, our not good enough ness, and simply keep speaking our misery into our life, even though it seems we have it all.

If I felt secure, safe, loved, worthy, and abundant deep inside within me, from me, about me, to me, would I speak anything opposite to this, or the antithesis of this? Would I complain and blame others and life for not giving me what I needed to feel loved and worthy?

Most of our words of blame are our projections from our beliefs.

Mirror, mirror of my life!

You are always speaking of what you yourself are creating. The loop of life is a bitch. And I say, "Life's a bitch until you make it your bitch."

To be conscious of your words means slowing down, seeing the mind, feeling the feelings, and watching the self, knowing the self, and being able to find that window where we don't react, or talk, or speak out our beliefs, and then course-correct and change them.

Conscious awareness is the key to changing life.

Folks will say, "I always do this. This always happens when . . ." Yup, you are asking and receiving and casting your spells again and again because you are make believing it to be so. The course-correct for this is a rephrase. Up until now, I used to blah blah.

Now we are changing the program and owning a new one and are aware of our words and magic. We can alter many of our words when we truly start to focus on our awareness of what they are saying about our beliefs. We speak about what the mirror shows us about us, then we loop life.

What is the mirror doing? It's reflecting us back to us. Wow. I'm speaking my beliefs into life, and life just confirms my beliefs. My core barriers of limiting beliefs, my unloved not good enough ness, drive the thoughts, feelings, and then words. I always speak about how I am, how I see life from my beliefs about me. Life reflects me back to me.

Two people can experience the same circumstances and see it in very different ways. They are waiting to meet someone, a friend. The friend is late. One man gets upset, angry, and says he feel disrespected. The other friend is also late. And his waiting buddy simply says, "Glad you made it," with no anger. How they were within them then comes out in their words. One man has an inner issue; he then creates life from within his loop. The other does the same from their perceptions. How we feel about ourselves, from our deep unknown, keeps showing us

161

to us. See, it's not the outside, its actually the lenses of perceptions and beliefs we see through.

Am I speaking a victim sentence? Am I seeing my deep, limiting, barriers of beliefs and not good enough ness being cast into spells?

If your partner triggers you, your stuff, you will normally say, "That makes me feel unhappy." You make me feel blah blah. Now you believe they did this, they got inside you, touched your sticky stuff of not good enough ness and triggered your ammunition and did that to you. And because you believe it, you say it. And of course, you keep believing it. The victim speaks their victim life into a loop and mirror. Ouch.

Or, another way, the way of the map, if, when triggered, I say, "I'm feeling a little triggered by your words. I have to have a moment to see what this is, work through this." You are now speaking from full responsibility, changing your beliefs that someone else did it, not getting into an argument of wounds, turning inward to see yourself, and so alter your whole beliefs, words, and then alter life. This is learning, like the rest of this book, to operate with a whole new language and perception.

Many people say, "My partner never listens."

These people's parents never listened to them, so they believe themselves unworthy, not good enough, neglected, not seen. And so, this belief plays out in thoughts and then words.

And because of this, maybe, you shout at your partner, scorn them, tell them, and trigger their parental wounds, which cause a trauma response of shutdown. Because when they were shouted at as children, they went into a freeze response to survive.

You keep creating from your beliefs and words that no one listens to you. If you could be gentle with your partner and express yourself differently, maybe you might feel heard.

"Life's always such a struggle."

This believes and speaks life's a struggle. And usually, this person simply keeps creating life so. Parents create a home of this energy. They speak of struggling. The child ingests it and believes in this hardship. And then they grow up and live this loop.

Or you could say, circumstances will always bring an amazing lesson to learn. And this person is always aware and growing, changing their beliefs, changing their words, using the map, and so life reflects this back.

Reframing our words is a whole new way of speaking. What are my words spelling out? What am I actually saying here that creates a loop I don't like? We simply never ever think of how we speak. We are never consciously aware. We dribble our magic spells blindly.

Using the words and sentences in a positive way alters our relationships with our relationship with life.

It's impossible to get a parking space. This person never gets a space.

Our deep beliefs drive our words, which cast our spells, which the mirror loops and reflects. The more we become aware of our words, of what they are actually spelling out, the more we alter our words, the more we alter our whole life.

I can't, won't.

I'm no good at that. Will remain so.

It's impossible, will never dare.

I'm possible, always dares.

I should, or have to do this or that, has an effort attached to it.

Our not good enough ness speaks itself into the loop of life, cementing the beliefs, and creating from that space and place. We can reframe everything if we slow down and build our awareness of our creative beliefs, thoughts, feelings, words, actions, inactions, and reactions.

The Loop of Life

Our barriers of beliefs, the bag of our unloved, not good enough ness, our sticky stuck stuff, are like prisons that blind us, that speak their words, stay where they believe, and never change from where they are. The loop of life is the same old same. How do we break the loop? We read this book again and again, become the change that changes our beliefs, do the work, moment to moment, and create a whole new loop that keeps expanding and elevating us and not going round and around constricting us. Most can't see past their beliefs; they simply moan and bitch and complain from them. Most don't want to change their loop because it's simply their addictive comfort zone. And to change our beliefs is like dying to who we have always been. People literally stay in the loop of their victim mentality because they have identified with it, to think and believe its who they are. We are nothing but a bunch of beliefs. If we keep believing it to be so, it will be so. If we keep being so, we become so.

The loop is an invisible weight, a darkness, built from our childhood. Our beliefs about our unworthiness, our unsafety, our undeserving, and how unloved and not good enough we feel, all loop life in the mirror of life to show us to us.

CHAPTER 14

Male and Female.
Conscious Subconscious

We interpreted and created beliefs and perceptions, as children, as best we could,
which had us thinking and believing
and speaking how we felt about life. These were our
seeds of our conscious, the male. They then fed and
seeded the female, the subconscious, our software
programs. The female subconscious births how we
are, how we feel, how we think, how we believe, how
we react, how we act, how we speak. Now we keep
seeding and feeding and creating who we are from
this birthing and creating machine of the loop of life.
If we don't become aware, these software conscious
and subconscious programs will run our whole life
continuously till we die. Most people will literally

believe the same beliefs, feel the same feelings, think the same thoughts, react with the same reactions, and speak the same words for most of their lives without any change. They live in the past their whole lives.

This is where the map changes everything. As we become more aware of our operating systems, more aware that we have been asleep at the wheel of life, recreating the past, we can start to strengthen our awareness and start to make the changes and become the change that changes us from the inside, and then this is reflected back to us in life.

Our whole life is in our hands. We birth what and how we are. We birth it knowingly, or not. We birth it from blind wounds, from traumas and a bag of unloved not good enough ness, or we operate from an awareness and constant change of course-correcting and healing.

Compassion and Forgiveness for the Self and All Else

Compassion, to me, is simply having a greater understanding for myself, and so for everyone else. If I see my blindness, I then see myself more, know myself more, and so know everyone else more. The more I become aware of the Map, the more I become aware of how lost and blind I was, the more compassion I find for myself, not beat myself up, not criticize myself, and so find grace for where I am on this amazing journey of discovery and self-inquiry.

This also then applies to having compassion for where everyone else is. This includes the past, our parents, our old partners, and anyone else we have any issues with or upset with. Remember, the issue is the issue I have about the issue, not the issue itself. If I can truly have a greater insight and see this, I can find the compassion and forgiveness for others. Others are doing their best where they are without the map, full of not good enough ness, full of blindness, full of pain and hurt, just as I have been.

The greatest compassion and forgiveness we know of in stories, the greatest example of how deep it can go, was the narrative of a man being nailed hands and feet to a cross with a crown of thorns on his head and then being stabbed with a spear. As his blood ran down his body he said, "Forgive them for they know not what they do."

I look back at my old self, my angry self, my words I have used, my passive-aggressiveness and spite, my want for violence and vengeance, and the blind bigotry and support for certain wars and oppressions against specific people, and I see the pain and hurt behind it all. I have compassion for my old self. I have forgiveness for all I was. This releases me from my self-criticisms and self-judgments, the guilt and shame I myself might carry, and carried once upon a time. I did as I did, from where I was. It was the me who stabbed myself with a spear. Compassion is a gift we give ourselves, especially for others. If we don't find compassion and forgiveness, what are we left with? Hurt and pain projecting as anger, spite, resentments, jealousy, vengefulness, unforgiving, hate, judgments, and all else of the disease and poison I keep swallowing and ingesting, by me, from me, from my inability to see this genius greater understanding.

When we find true deeper compassion, we can release energy, cry, and even wail. When we truly find the forgiveness for others we can soften and cry with the release of all the disease we have held in the past. We can continually liberate ourselves from the chains we have imprisoned ourselves in. It is we who hold our ill feelings. It is we who suffer from them.

It is we who eat ourselves alive, carry the weight and darkness and bitterness our whole life. It is also we who can unload this baggage and darkness.

The courage to find compassion is moving out of our head and into our hearts. This is one of the most courageous journeys to take. The head has been protecting our heart due to all the hurt and pain from childhood. And so, we guard ourselves and protect ourselves and close our heart. We blame and complain from our head not to face our pain, not to be vulnerable enough to enter the courage of the hero's heart. Again, the word "courage" comes from the French word *Coeur*, meaning heart. And courage is one step over fear. Our fear is of being hurt again. So, we close out heart to protect our heart and live in constant fear. That is the obviousness of how not to live in love. The Map is basically a way of opening up the heart bit by bit, again and again, by dissolving and resolving all the head-created beliefs of our unloved pain.

The Nervous System

I have expressed the womb experience. How our mother was, how her relationship with her partner was, and how it affects the child inside. We share her nervous energy and chemical soup to form our biological and physiological underbelly and operating systems. Our nervous system is already being formed pre-birth.

Then we enter into the world, and our varying degrees of feeling unsafe, our fight or flight systems of fear and survival due to our home environment, add and create more layers. Of course, due to the nuclear family and patriarchy, we are not attended to like the community or tribe from day one. We then suffer the energetic of more stress, frustration, anxiety, impatience, loud and tense tones, and much else that is deemed and seen as a normal environment. It's not. Depending on the family home and dynamic, a child's nervous system is affected by many ways and by varying degrees. Simply being left to cry and not being attended to from a few seconds to a few minutes or longer can create a mild to heavy trauma response in the body that ramps up the unsafe feelings inside. If there is loud friction, effects of addictions, tensions, shouting at other children, or shouting in general, the child ingests all these energetics. Our nervous system is doing its best to survive and feel safe. We can only rely on our home and parents and siblings to feel safe.

Even if a parent is engaged with a screen, a TV, a phone, we are now not being attended to, and we feel mild to medium abandonment. We are not as important. We are not enough for their attention. A baby's natural status is to be held for most of its first two years, slept with, mostly attended to and looked after, and fully loved by many of the tribe or village environment. The nuclear family utterly diminishes this amount of required attention and natural nurturing.

We are perpetually on guard, unsafe.

If a small child is out with the parent and is in a pushchair, it is already now disconnected to the parent's body, eye level and view. They are literally operating alone, near the ground, when they have become accustomed to being held. We are now being pushed around in strange places detached from our safe place, which is with the parent, close to the body and heartbeat. This is also a mild abandonment. The child might also feel restricted, confined, and want to get out, this also affects their nervous system. They are strapped in, held down. This is not their normal running around naked in nature. Then, they might be told to be quiet and to behave because the parent wants them to be how they want in public, out and about. The parent is not meeting the child's natural freedom. They will then feel some tension and frustration, which translates as unsafe. So many tiny, every day, simple, seemingly normal behaviors all add up to cause an effect in the nervous system of a small child. This is all part of the ten thousand wounds. A child takes in how to communicate and much else from being held by the parent and being at their level of relating. This is how they can learn more of how to relate to, and with, the world and others. The child will watch and see and learn from this vantage point. In a pushchair they see knees. We take that extra learning of communication and closeness out of the picture. But it is far easier and much more convenient to do the pushchair.

There is no wrong or right. We simply became this system of operating. And this is simply showing what we have normalized, when in fact it can cause many unknown effects.

For at least a few hundred thousand years we were hunter-gatherers. We were held with the mother much of the time, or other adults. If not, we were simply outside and with a range of older children and not just stuck with a bunch of our immature peers. We were never restricted in car seat or pushchairs and hushed up, shut up, and forced to behave and restrain our nature. A child is loud and full of the imagination and inquiry of its nature. Being told to be quiet is for the parent. I get it. I understand it. I am simply expressing what all of us experienced and the effects it adds up to on our nervous system, which then rules our lives.

We are literally restraining our babies, young children, and squashing their nature, their vitality, their imaginations. Their nervous system becomes nervous, in fight or flight, unsafe, and utterly dysregulated. Then we are stuck in front of screens, not in nature, our nature, and our nervous system plugs into this fake overstimulation of unnatural functioning. Already the child is living in a constant assault on its natural needs and tendencies to fit into our seeming normality.

Now squash them into the pressure to perform for validation at home, to get love, a cookie, gold stars at school, grades at high school, peer pressure, and all else the media shoves at them, and they are programmed to constantly keep up, catch up, seek safety, and therefore feel unsafe in some form of having to behave and be how others want them to be. This all adds up to one and one makes unsafe, neurosis, unsafe, insecure, anxiety, unsafe, and a ton else that affects the nervous system now forming into its default autopilot software programs. What a cluster fuck we are all perfectly raised into. This is just the tip of the iceberg.

Take this, imagine this for a little child, and now see how this carries into our whole life with added constants from peer pressure, parental pressures, media comparisons, and a general boost of not good enough ness to feed the system into a constant of restlessness, unease, disease, and a need for sooth-ing, stimulation, distractions, sedations, validations, and instant gratifications. Our whole body is being flooded with chemicals of survival and dysregulation. Our immune system, bodies, and minds are not built for this.

We are now programmed and deeply conditioned out of our unconditional and into a normal state of an unsafe need, mild to heavy anxiety, impatience, restlessness, neurosis, and all else that discomforts our norms. Then our children get labeled, shoved with mafia medicine pills, and off you go. We shallow breathe, live in a constant feeling of lack, of not good enough ness, and can never rest unless we are seeking some form of soothing or are asleep.

We are habitually in a familiar unsafe fight or flight space within. Most who go to nature find quiet and have no distraction or stimulation and will feel a discomfort, feel unsafe, without even knowing it. Folks ask where my TV is. I don't have one, or a Netflix or any other payment subscription so I can watch the media. I spend much of my time writing, reading, in silence, in nature, gardening, and keeping my system regulated and at peace. I lived in mayhem for much of my life. It's fucking insanity how we have made a normality of constant overstimulation.

What is actually a feeling of safe, for the nervous system, is what is familiar. We unknowingly seek the overstimulation, frantic lover, angry lover, impatient lover, or anything else that mirrors how we were raised. We literally attract and match all we actually don't want. It matches our old mayhem, our old dysfunction, rather than find us some peace and deeper love. We attract and match and seek out what our nervous system tells us.

Turn on the screen, scroll, eat, go to a noisy place, eat, find crowds, or take some substance or any other soothing to try to calm the constant of our constantly contributing to our dysregulation. We cause it, then try to soothe it. We are now in the loop of life. It's utterly insane. It's a major cause for the body saying fuck this, I can't cope, and it screams in many ways to show us our dis ease.

This is an underbelly that rules us invisibly. This is our very nervous, anxious nervous system of the normality of humanity. OOF.

What Do We Do to Regulate?

When we feel anxious, nervous, impatient, frustrated, insecure, unsafe, those familiar feelings of restlessness, or we seek to soothe because we can't sit with our self, we immediately have to become aware that we are now operating on a default loop of how we have always been. We are feeding the beast, the machine of the programmed past.

We must see this and be able to detach from our old self that is looping life into the same old same.

It's very much like a trigger reaction, but our inner self causes a need for more of the same old same chemicals of pain, that loop the loop and keep the nervous system feeling familiar in its dysregulation.

Mind the Gap!

We need to see that we need to create a gap, a space, to disrupt the old loop.

We normally unconsciously repeat the same unconscious, subconscious patterns of feelings and thoughts, actions and reactions and inactions, shallow breathing, words, and all else we have always operated from. We run on an old software program of us. It seems like this is who we are, but it's not. It's a habitual formation and constructed addiction of our unawareness.

Without awareness, we remain in the unaware loop, constantly repeating and recreating and cementing who we are, who we think we are, who we believe ourselves to be. We keep feeling the same story, thinking the same story, being anxious the same way, being impatient the same way, and all else the same old same, of the same old software.

We live in the past.

We state our state into the statement of our lives, perpetuating our state, cementing our state, creating our state, make believing, feeling, thinking, and speaking our state into the loop of life.

Therefore, to break the loop, to start to change the same old same, we must see it's not who we are, see it's an old story, an old state we are stating, thinking and feeling, and catch ourselves before we fall into the spell of our old ego patterns and feed our nervous system more of the same.

The software can't be updated if I don't know it is old, and don't update it.

Literally everything that upsets me and disturbs me is for me to see, for me to feel, for me to move through and heal. All my judgments and complaints and blames are all poisons of the past programs I repeat. I am in a constant of unacceptability, resistance, fight or flight. I eat, seed, and feed, and repeat my same old same. If I were the new me, wouldn't it be nice to accept others, see them how they are, have compassion for them, and then not fall into my own disease of the opposite? If I were the new me, an updated software of me, wouldn't it be far nicer, more peaceful, and more loving to me not to get upset and disturbed from the outside or from within? If I were the new me, wouldn't it be nice to see my belittling beliefs, not allow them to play out, rule me and fool me, and do the inner child work? You see where this can go?

Anxiety, frustration, impatience, restlessness, and our general constant disease that we create are all open to change. That being said, how many opportunities are we being presented with to course-correct, to update our old software, to resolve and dissolve the old beliefs and bring about new ones, more loving and abundant ones? It's amazing how much we can keep becoming the change. It's a full school load of homework to work with, moment to moment.

I am in conscious awareness, watching myself all the time. It's now mostly second nature. But this has become a process to become so. The old self does not want you to become aware, because it then knows its days are numbered, it can't feed and seed its addiction and suffering.

If I have feelings, thoughts, reactions, anxiety, impatience, insecurity, and limiting beliefs, are they who I am? NO! I have them. I created them. I believe they are me and think I am them. This is me being stuck in my unaware loop of me.

181

In actuality, I am the subject, and they are the objects of my awareness. Or should I say, my unawareness.

This has to be truly known of the self, known by thyself to know thyself, for the change to start to reprogram and reseed and feed the systems in place. I am not this reaction, this thought, or this feeling. They are showing me to me for me to see this. Or they are simply going to go unnoticed, and I repeat the programs and loop myself into my loopy self-suffering.

Hopefully, you are now quite aware of your normal unawareness. Funny enough, this is quite abnormal by normal standards.

This is paramount. Conscious awareness is the key to opening the door to a whole new space and place within. From this constant awareness of watching the self, we can then begin to see our old self and not buy into the old narratives and stories, not attach to the same feelings, not believe the same beliefs, and not react to the same reactions of our bad actor, or allow the tsunami of old chemicals, neurological pathways, subconscious loops, and nervous system rulers to rule over us. To enter the kingdom within, to sit on our own throne and rule, we have to do this hero's work and rescue us from our constant victim and its blindness. Bless my little victim. He did a good job. But he overstayed his welcome.

I must now take my power back, rise above my old self, and not fall back into its grip. This is the moment to moment of the work. The more we work the more the pay. And the pay is more compassion, love, forgiveness, understanding, and peace.

It's not a simple task to learn a new language of life, to die to our past. We have lived these habits and addiction our whole life. Meditation will always show us how programmed we are. That's basically what it does. We sit and become aware of our stuff, but we do not get stuck to the stuff. And this is what it's all about—not being stuck in all the old sticky stuff of us. This is an all-day moment to moment practice and process.

Altering Our Behaviors

We feel whatever comes up and we shine our awareness onto it and see it as part of our old self, our old stuff, our old software programs. Now, in an instant I am already not lost in it or blinded by it. Now I see it. It's simply just an old habit trying to grab me into its loop.

A feeling arises, a thought, an anxiousness, an impatience— whatever it is, we feel it, it disturbs us. The space, the gap in between the feeling and us getting caught in it, is the brilliant and magical window of opportunity. It does not have to be an outside stimulus. Our dis ease and restless mess inside mostly plays itself out like an addict getting a fix of physiological chemicals whenever it decides to arise.

EXAMPLE

Here's an upsetting or disturbing feeling.

ALERT

I'm now more consciously aware. I'm the watcher of me.

I see that it's an old part of me.

I'm aware that I'm not that person.

I will detach and watch it, see it, feel it, and move through it without becoming it.

I will immediately take slower, deeper, breaths.

I will remind me that I am not the thought or feeling, not the beliefs, not the narrative, and I will continue to shine this light of awareness onto it and into it.

I focus on in and not getting caught in it.

I'm not seeding and feeding it.

Once I'm aware I can sit with it, in it, and be with it, and move into it and through it. This can be the toughest part, not to fall into the victim. Stay with it, be with it, watch it, move into it and through it, and allow it to take its time to diminish. I am in control of it—it is not in control of me. In time, with practice, you will see it loses power and starts to dissolve.

Again and again, I can now take my power back over my old self, my old loop, my old patterns and programs, and so don't give in to the old software version of my old self-suffering.

This can happen all day long. We might forget sometimes, but the very fact we get disturbed will bring us back to remember. We are learning a whole new operating system, navigation and translation, a whole new language of life, of us.

The old self does not wish to dissolve, weaken, or die. It's got power. This is the alchemy. We take the power of how we used to feed it, get caught up in it, and we turn it around and shine the light of our awareness onto it, feel it, and move through it.

We become so consciously aware that the power

of our old systems can't fool us, blind us, and get us to attach and loop the loop of our old life.

This is a new practice. And it is a process. Enlightening the self has no destination, no rules, no rush—it is simply a journey. Don't beat yourself up for not being better than you could be. You are utterly and perfectly you, where you are, where you are meant to be. And that's how we should remember our moments to be. That in itself is a mantra.

The Triggers Are the past.

We have accumulated ammunition over our life due to our inability to operate and navigate with the map. Our barriers of limiting beliefs, our bag of unloved not good enough ness, our labeled traumas, wounds, what some call samskaras, our labeled karma, are all stuck inside waiting for us to use the map and translate, navigate, resolve and dissolve them and the past, to process the wonderful journey back to the unconditional. It took you a lifetime to get to this understanding, where you are, in this moment, to come to this book, and so you have lived perfectly practiced in the other understandings. This is a discipline. You are the disciple of you, your temple.

CHAPTER 15

Soothing Is Not Healing

Soothing is not healing. We have a thousand ways not to do this work, not to face our pain. We distract and sedate and stimulate all day long. We are escape artists. The more we escape, the less we can build strength in our awareness, our ability to face the pain, to move through it, and heal it. This is the choice. The victim hides and seeks for soothing from their pain, in all it can, with whoever it can find, and wherever it can escape. The hero does not reach, crutch, use, or hide or seek. The hero faces itself. Soothing is satiation, not salvation. We either chase the dragon of our victim in soothing our whole life or rise and rise into our hero's glory. It's simply a choice of discipline.

I know it's not easy. The urge to soothe, sedate,

distract, and escape is a lifelong habit. We are literally escape addicts. It's our default setting from when we got our sugary treat and got dumped in front of the TV. Facing the pain is unfamiliar and our whole system will try not to feel the pain.

If pain is soothed, it's not healed. It just keeps seeking soothing. The ego is very smart.

But once upon a time, the little baby of you decided to walk. You bumped your head, elbow, and knee again and again and cried, fell down, got up, fell down, got up, cried, and got up and fell, and wobbled. And soon enough it all became second nature. I remember trying to tie my shoelaces. I remember many things that were not easy. Of course, we have a lifetime of habit and addiction to our loop to break and contend with. This is the great experience of the journey, to become this hero, to climb the mountain of us. I was who I was and have become who I am. I am always in the work, consciously aware. I never ever used to be this person. I am no different to anyone. I had enough of pretending I was happy, soothing, being angry and projecting, and not facing myself. My whole life is beyond better than I could ever have imagined, and it's not attached to or dependent and reliant on anything or anyone else for my peace, love, inner wealth, and deep happiness of being.

Take steps to reduce all aspects of your soothing. We reach, and crutch and use, all the time. Social media and the screens are just as insidious and addictive as heroin these days. Add up the time wasted on line, and you could have read this book ten times in a few months and truly ingested the information and be well on your way to your digesting and embodying a hero's journey. I was addicted to seminars, to courses, to swallowing information up. It's always good to learn. And yet, this also becomes a bypass of sitting in our stuff and moving through. Find nature, move daily, find silence, and breathe deeply and slowly as much as you can. Make it a new habit. These on their own are the antithesis of our unease and restlessness. It is essential to give us gifts of peace instead of gifts of soothing. They are very subtly the same and yet incredibly different.

The only way is through. All else is a scenic escape route, a distraction from facing ourselves.

Opportunity to Be the Change Is Everywhere

We are constantly presented with chances moment to moment to alter our past in the present moment. Every trigger, upset, and disturbance is there for us to see, to feel, to move into and through and heal. Every time we belittle ourselves, berate ourselves, judge and criticize ourselves, we can see this as our little child caught in its old story of its beliefs and bag of not good enough ness. We can be there and course-correct, speak to our little child, and bring love to these unloved parts, again and again. I am always there for my little boy. I am always using my slow and deeper breaths to regulate myself to calmer levels. I am always in my conscious awareness because I have practiced it to this second nature.

When I am there for my little child inside, I use a soft tone, a patient tone, a compassionate heart.

These are some sentences we can use for our child. I am the greatest parent to me.

I'm here for you.

I've got you.

It's ok.

We're going to do this together.

It's just an old story. We're making a new one.

How do you feel?

I'm here. I love you.

We're so amazing and brilliant.

It's ok.

When we feel hurt or in pain, alone, we can speak to this inner pain, our inner child, and ask it how it feels. This is bringing love to the pain of what we have labeled as loneliness. Loneliness is what we do with being alone. Alone is a stunning place to be, when we have done the work. It's the ultimate luxury. There is a little child inside who was never met, never seen, or heard for them. This is healing the pain of the past in the present.

Breath is the key to regulating our self. It's free. Box breath is wonderful to meditate for a few minutes or more.

Four seconds breathing in slowly.

Hold for four seconds.

Breathe out slowly for four seconds.

Hold the breath for four seconds.

And keep this going.

It eases and stops the mind from its mad monkey, from its anxious ramblings. There are many forms of breath work. The simple, slow, and deep belly breaths are perfect for use in the car, watching TV, when anything upsets or triggers us. The more we utilize this, the more we can become habitual about its ease of use. I am very much using this brilliant form of constantly regulating my nervous system. It literally resets our whole mind and body from a whole life of the opposite.

The discipline of life is the key to life. We are our own temple. Our mental, emotional, physical, biological, physiological, and spiritual well-being are all ours to keep as we keep them. And it is we who are the cause and effect of them all.

We are the constant victim of our choices, or we are the constant hero of our choices.

Nurturing Peace

Learning to be alone with the self is very important. So is learning to find silence and be in nature as much as possible. Turn off the machines two hours before bed. No screens. This is imperative to alter our sleep and break our habits as well as set discipline. In the morning, do not start the day with a screen for as long as possible. Start with you. Sing affirming songs or mantras. Move. Breathe. Give the gift of the new day, a breaking of the old habit and creating a new. This is the essence of what we are doing. The map is bringing us back.

Before we drift off to sleep, and just before we open our eyes in the morning are powerful times for prayers and affirmations. Here are some I use as my ritual and discipline. Why take your crap to bed to wake up to crap? We must feel these words, be these words, and own their being and not just say them.

The feeling is the most important. Imagination is a huge key to creation. In the image of. We must find the place and space within us of gratitude, abundance, and love. This is simply creating a feeling inside to embody the words. This is also something to mediate with and slowly breathe.

Thank you for resolving all that needed to be resolved.

Say these five to ten times.

This is taking the worry and anxiety out of things uncertain, unresolved, and unknown. It literally brings an opposite to our system.

I am that I am. And I am enough.

Say these five to ten times.

This is the antithesis of our programmed not good enough ness.

Thank you for the health, the love, the success, and the wealth.

Say this ten times.

This gratitude for a perfect way of being and living is the medicine. I use this all day long.

I use these constantly whenever I feel I could alter my feelings. We have belittled ourselves and worried and been in scarcity our whole lives, constantly reaffirming with words and feelings. We can't change unless we believe we can change. And without knowing the beliefs we have been living under, we won't be able to change them. They will work like spies.

We can't change if we keep playing the same tunes and reacting with the same reacts and being the same impatience and being the same frustration and all else. We have to be the most aware and loving self to ourselves to bring us back to love. And as we do this, life feels more loving and easier, and then life reflects this. This is a process. Do not seek for results, or want rewards, or be expecting. That in itself is counteractive and adds to a feeling of not good enough ness. See how that works? Come on, I'm not enlightened enough yet. Having compassion for your journey is key to the journey and keeps it moving in the right direction. Be gentle and kind with you. This is the parent we wanted, the love we crave, the healing we require.

For the hero, life is happening for us to clear the lenses of our perceptions. The victim thinks life is happening to them, or against them. It is a constant moment to moment of potential growth and change, of evolving out of our old self, elevating into the higher self. The Map is a simple understanding of how to navigate and translate and operate life. As we become more familiar with using the tools and ways, we map a new destiny, a whole new future by healing our past.

I have given you the best possible explanation of all my work, my twenty years of undoing my own darkness, of putting down my own baggage of my own weight, of my enlightening journey from the darkness of my past to this beautiful loving and compassionate place I now live in. It continues always, and life brilliantly brings me new opportunities in every moment. We are all full of love and wisdom.

We simply got smothered in our unloved not good enough ness and have been externalizing life to try to soothe or overcompensate.

To be in this world, but not of this world. Some little brown Palestinian Jew said this 2,000 years ago.

"Nothing is real, nothing to get hung about," said the Beatles 2,000 years later, to the day.

These sentences are expressing the same thing to me. We can live in peace and love regardless of.

There is no loss in life, just love. There is only me in here, with me, within. They say we are all one, all connected, all of the source of creation. I am, you are, we are love. And it is simply the journey of shedding all that is not love, by using all that is not love, to get back to love.

I've had mild fame and fortune and been utterly miserable in my unloved not good enough ness. In my private work I work with successful and married people all suffering their own inner sticky stuff. Don't compare yourself to the show and tell of the show and sell you see. Many who look happy and enough are far from it. This work is the ability to self-inquire, to assist yourselves, to be a constant personal assistant to bringing you back to wealth and love and safety within. I have playfully given myself the label of The Evolutionist. And that's what this is. The first four letters of that word spell "love" backwards. We are evolving back to our truth that will set us free of our old, imprisoned, blindness and suffering. I promise you, if you truly face yourself and become disciplined in this way of operating, have compassion and a greater understanding that everyone is operating without this understanding, you will feel the changes. This is not a fad, a destination, or a result—it is learning a new language, a new translation and navigation of life.

A man called Osho once told this story. You sit at the circus, waiting excitedly for the next act as the music and lights prepare you. The curtains open and out comes a man standing astride two horses. Wow! No ropes or safety net. The horses move with pace around the circus ring as he perfectly balances one leg on each. They are not tethered together, and yet run together in unison. This is what we are learning with the Map. We are learning to ride our life and at the same time become a whole different person, living another life while doing so. This man on the horses had to practice becoming so at ease. He once had an idea. He then found a map, a way, and he took his patient time to figure out the balance. He fell off, slipped, bumped, stumbled, and even cut himself now and then. At first, he had safety ropes and eventually took them away and became more courageous, determined, and inspired by his very own progress.

This journey is a journey, a process. We will enlighten and soften from who we were. We will evolve into a new person, bit by bit. We will notice we react less, find peace more. It can become a whole new addiction. Do not try to force this onto anyone else. You may express to them what you are doing. Everyone is where they are. And this must be respected and understood. Many people find their way when they do, if they do. It is up to them to come to this new learning. This is our own greatest part of all of this. We are gaining sight while many around us won't be. This is respecting them for where they are, meeting them where they are, and not thinking yourself better for where you are. Remember, you were once where they are. So, they can also take the journey any time.

A genius. The genie of us. We are all unique and brilliant individuals with our very own genie of us.

The cork was put in by us, by our limiting barriers of belief. This is a choice to create a more magical life. You hold all the power to find more peace and love.

Thank you for finding the Map. It was an idea that came to me from a very distinct voice. And I sat with it and let it go. Then in my sleep a very strong voice said it was time to bring this book to actuality. That is the magic.

Evolve with love and compassion.

I wish you all the courage, discipline, and determination for your new hero's journey. As you travel you will meet new people traveling with you. Maybe you can create some Map meetings in certain areas near where you live. That would be wonderful for people to assist each other and share their thoughts and ideas. You create a like-minded community.

"Be the change you wish to see in the world." The great quote by Gandhi. This is what we are doing by this work. The world needs us to heal the past and to be this change.

Love is the greatest force and power. It is literally almighty.

Sending you all the love.

Thank you.

Some books I love

The Power of Now
Eckhart Tolle

A New Earth
Eckhart Tolle

The Untethered Soul
Michael Singer

You Are the One You've Been Waiting For
Richard C. Schwartz

To Be a Man
Robert Augustus Masters

Getting the Love you Want
Harville Hendrix & Helen LaKelly Hunt

The Honeymoon Effect
Bruce Lipton

The Biology of Belief
Bruce Lipton

Breaking the Habit of Being Yourself,
Joe Dispenza

You are on the hero's journey of awakening, in the school of life, strengthening your conscious awareness, clearing the lenses of your perceptions, healing your old wounds from childhood, dissolving and resolving your barriers of limiting beliefs, finding more compassion and forgiveness for yourself and others, coming into a much deeper and greater understanding, enlightening yourself of your old, unloved, not good enough ness, and so living with far more peace and love.

We are rebels in the revolution of the evolution of consciousness.

LOVE
Living Our Very Essence.

Made in the USA
Monee, IL
06 December 2024

72637992R00127